Traditions in

LITERATURE

AMERICA READS   **CLASSIC EDITION**

STUDY GUIDES

to accompany
Traditions in Literature

CLASSIC
EDITION
S F

SCOTT, FORESMAN

Scott, Foresman and Company
Editorial Offices: Glenview, Illinois

Regional Offices: Sunnyvale, California ●
Tucker, Georgia ● Glenview, Illinois ●
Oakland, New Jersey ● Dallas, Texas

Preface

These **Study Guides** are intended to help you provide for the abilities of all students. Step-by-step questions are to be answered on the *Study Guide* page as a student reads a selection independently. For students in the lower half of your class, the *Study Guides* will be useful in bringing them to the point where they can discuss a selection in class. With many selections, however, you will want to assign *Study Guides* to the whole class. This work is not intended to be graded, but you may want to check from time to time to see that students are using them profitably.

ISBN: 0-673-27138-2

Copyright © 1989 Scott, Foresman and Company
All Rights Reserved
Printed in the United States of America

2345678910-MAL-989796959493929190898 8

Contents

Name   Class   Date

The Conjurer's Revenge
by Stephen Leacock

Beginning the Story

Read the story up to the end of the third paragraph on page 4, at which point the conjurer has produced everything from a bowl of gold-fish to a rocking-chair.

1. What is another word for *conjurer*?

_____

2. What do people say after his first trick?

_____

3. How does the Quick Man explain each of the conjurer's tricks?

_____

4. How does the audience react to other tricks of the conjurer?

_____

5. What has happened to the conjurer's reputation?

_____

Continuing the Story

Continue reading to the end of the story, answering the questions below.

6. For his last trick, the conjurer borrows several things from the Quick Man. What are they, and what does he do to each of them?

_____

_____

_____

7. Why is the Quick Man happy to allow him to take his belongings?

_____

_____

8. How has the conjurer tricked the Quick Man?

_____

Thinking About the Story

9. Do you think the conjurer was right to get revenge on the Quick Man? Explain your answer.

_____

_____

_____

_____

_____

_____

_____

_____

Copyright © Scott, Foresman and Company

1

Name	Class	Date

The Monkey's Paw
by W. W. Jacobs

Beginning the Story
As you read the story, notice the effect the monkey's paw has on each character. Stop at the space on page 10, column 2.

1. Describe the small parlor in Lakesnam Villa and the people in it.

_____

_____

_____

2. What does Mr. White complain about so violently, and what does his wife think he's really angry about?

_____

_____

_____

3. How does the White family treat Sergeant-Major Morris? Explain your answer.

_____

_____

4. How do Mr. White and Sergeant-Major Morris know one another?

_____

5. Why did the Indian fakir put the spell on the monkey's paw?

_____

_____

6. What does Morris more than once urge White to do with the monkey's paw?

_____

7. What does Mr. White wish for, and who suggests that he wish for it?

_____

8. Why does the old man give "a shuddering cry" just as he finishes the wish?

_____

_____

Continuing the Story
Continue reading until the next space in the story on page 12, column 1.

9. Although Mr. White makes the first wish, and neither his wife nor Herbert will admit that the paw moved, who becomes most interested in the outcome of their experiment?

_____

10. Why does Mr. White faint when he learns the amount Maw and Meggins plan to give them as compensation?

_____

_____

Name   Class   Date

Continue reading to the end of the story.

11. Choose one sentence from the first two paragraphs of this last section of the story that shows how the Whites have adjusted to their son's death.

_____

_____

12. What does Mrs. White decide they must wish for the second time?

_____

13. What is Mr. Smith's reaction to her plan?

_____

14. Why does the paw fall to the floor and Mr. White regard it "shudderingly?"

_____

15. What did Mrs. White forget "was two miles away"?

_____

16. What do you assume is Mr. White's last wish?

_____

17. Why do you think he makes that wish?

_____

_____

Thinking About the Story

18. Has Mr. White's last wish put an end to the curse? Why or why not?

_____

_____

_____

_____

_____

_____

_____

Name   Class   Date

The Adventure of the Blue Carbuncle
by Arthur Conan Doyle

Beginning the Story

As in any Sherlock Holmes tale, in this story the reader must learn to juggle many distinct pieces of information. No individual piece is difficult to understand, but fitting them all together is often bewildering. As you read Dr. Watson's account, stop at each new fact for a moment. Read slowly up to the point at the bottom of page 21, column 1, where Holmes says, "I suppose you know what you have got?"

1. Holmes relates to Watson the circumstances that brought the battered hat into his possession. Tell this incident in your own words. Be as brief as you can.

_____

_____

_____

_____

2. List three features of the battered hat, and their significance, as Holmes paints his portrait of Henry Baker for Watson.

FEATURE: **SIGNIFICANCE:**

_____   _____

_____   _____

_____   _____

3. How does Holmes deduce that the man was bringing the goose to his wife as a peace offering?

_____

_____

4. Peterson bursts into Holmes's apartment with something in his hand. What is it, and where was it found?

_____

_____

Continuing the Story

Continue reading to the end of the paragraph in which Holmes invites Watson to dine with him at seven, page 23, column 2.

5. How much money is the Countess of Morcar's blue carbuncle worth?

_____

6. As briefly as possible, tell how the newspaper reports the carbuncle was stolen.

_____

_____

_____

_____

Name   Class   Date

7. What did Holmes learn about Henry Baker, by analyzing his hat, which now convinces the detective that a lost-and-found ad in the afternoon newspapers will bring Baker to him?

8. Holmes refers to the carbuncle as a "nucleus and focus of crime," then goes on to give an account of its history. How old is the stone, and where was it found?

Continue reading to the end of the paragraph on page 27, column 1, that begins "Ha! this may save us a visit to Brixton Road . . . ."

9. Fill in the most important detail that each of the following characters contributes to the plot:

Henry Baker _____

Alpha Inn landlord _____

Breckinridge _____

10. What about Breckinridge makes Holmes feel that he can draw him into a bet?

Continue reading to the end of the story.

11. Who told Ryder about the stone in the Countess's room?

12. As Holmes coaxes the truth out of James Ryder, what piece of information intrigues him most?

13. What reason does Holmes give for protecting Ryder from the police?

Thinking About the Story

14. Put yourself in the place of John Horner, the man who was falsely accused of stealing the blue carbuncle. Write a short account of the events leading up to the robbery from Horner's perspective.

6

Name   Class   Date

The Parachutist
by D'Arcy Niland

Carefully read the title and the quotation before beginning the story. Now read the story straight through to the end. Notice how the author gives character to the two animals, even though they cannot speak.

1. Why is the hawk starving?

_____

2. What does the author suggest about the hawk by saying it had a "practiced eye" and "scrutinized" its surroundings?

_____

3. Find the sentence that first mentions the kitten. How does the kitten's behavior differ from the hawk's?

_____

_____

4. Does the kitten seem fearful as the hawk swoops down on it? Support your answer.

_____

5. As the hawk carries the kitten higher and higher into "the heart of space," what does the kitten come to realize about its position?

_____

6. The kitten is described first as a parachutist, then as a pilot. Why?

_____

_____

7. What does the very last sentence of the story suggest about the kitten's awareness of what has just taken place?

_____

_____

Thinking About the Story
8. Do you think it was a good idea to have a kitten as the hawk's prey? Explain.

_____

_____

_____

9. Do you think a hawk can "hate"? Give reasons to support your answer.

_____

_____

_____

_____

Name   Class   Date

The Secret Life of Walter Mitty
by James Thurber

Beginning the Story

   Scenes change often and without warning in this story. As you read, note the details that point the story in a new direction. Stop at the end of the operating room episode on page 42, column 1.

   1. In the first paragraph, Walter Mitty imagines himself as the commander of a Navy hydroplane. What effect does this have on what he's *really* doing?

   _____

   2. Who brings Mitty out of this initial daydream?

   _____

   3. Thurber never reveals Mitty's real occupation. Why do you think it is better that you are without this information? What occupation would you assign to Walter Mitty?

   _____

   _____

   _____

   4. Why does Mitty fantasize the name Renshaw in the operating room episode?

   _____

   5. Who is Wellington McMillan, and who is his close personal friend?

   _____

   _____

   6. At one point during the operation fantasy, Dr. Renshaw says, "Coreopsis has set in." Why is this phrase funny? (Look up *coreopsis* in the dictionary for help.)

   _____

Continuing the Story

   Continue reading to the end of the story. Look for details that help you to complete your impression of the *real* Walter Mitty.

   7. Does Mitty's memory of removing tire chains from his car change in any way your impression of Mrs. Mitty? If so, how?

   _____

   _____

   8. In paragraph 2, page 42, Walter Mitty has forgotten "the what's-its-name." Find the statement that links the following courtroom scene to the forgotten item.

   _____

   9. Mitty finally remembers that "the what's-its-name" his wife asked him to buy is puppy biscuit. What jogs Mitty's memory?

   10. What sound effect does Thurber use more than once during the story to emphasize the silliness of Walter Mitty's fantasies?

   _____

Name   Class   Date

11. When Mr. and Mrs. Mitty meet again toward the end of the story, what does Mrs. Mitty say that shows she is rarely satisfied with her husband?

_____

_____

_____

_____

_____

Thinking About the Story

12. What do all of Walter Mitty's fantasy occupations have in common?

_____

_____

_____

_____

_____

13. What is Walter Mitty's last fantasy? Do you think he will go on to have others? Why or why not?

_____

_____

_____

_____

_____

_____

14. This is a very famous story, and the name Walter Mitty has even entered the dictionary. Why do you suppose this story is so popular?

_____

_____

_____

_____

_____

Name   Class   Date

A Visit to Grandmother
by William Melvin Kelley

Beginning the Story

Take careful note of the differences between Dr. Dunford and GL that emerge during the story. Read to the end of the paragraph that finds Dr. Dunford "sitting in the parlor while his mother spoke with her guests," on page 49, column 1.

1. Choose several words or phrases from the first paragraph that describe Chig's image of his father.

_____

2. What reasons does Dr. Dunford give for leaving home at fifteen years of age?

_____

_____

3. What kind of reception does Mama give her son Charles?

_____

4. Find one sentence that shows Mama is a strong and independent woman.

_____

_____

5. At the end of this section of the story, find a sentence that tells you how Charles Dunford related to his mother as a child.

_____

_____

Continuing the Story

Continue reading to the end of the story. Pay close attention to the character of GL, Dr. Dunford's brother.

6. Who is the older of the two sons, Charles or GL?

_____

7. What is your first impression of GL as the family begins to speak about him?

_____

8. Was GL's transaction with the horse trader fair?

_____

9. When Mama tells GL to take the horse back, what reason does he give for not doing so?

_____

_____

10. To what does Mama attribute the change in the horse's behavior?

_____

_____

11. Why do you think Mama rides with GL against her better judgment?

_____

12. What comment does Mama make about stopping the runaway horse that reveals her attitude toward her children?

_____

_____

13. What bothers Charles most about GL and Mama's horse episode?

_____

14. How does Charles Dunford react to Mama's declaration that she loved all of her children equally?

_____

15. Does GL's entrance at the end of the story reinforce Dr. Dunford's understanding of the past or Mama's? Why?

_____

_____

Thinking About the Story

16. Look at your answer to question 1. How do you think Dr. Dunford's relationship with his mother contributed to forming his manner of relating to other people?

_____

_____

_____

17. When Mama realizes what is wrong with Charles, she tries to reassure him of her love. Her son says, however, that it is too late. For what, in Charles's opinion, is it too late? Do you agree?

_____

_____

_____

The Other Wife
by Colette

Beginning the Story

Read the title and quotation on page 54. As you move through the story, look for ways in which the two wives differ. Read up to the point at which Marc Séguy expresses his relief that his divorce has not produced "any guilty parties or victims!" (page 55, column 1)

1. As the story opens, does Alice or Marc feel more at ease in the restaurant? Find two sentences that show which character is uncomfortable.

_____

_____

_____

2. Who does Marc recognize in the restaurant?

_____

3. What reason does Marc give for his divorce?

_____

Continuing the Story

Continue reading to the end of the story.

4. Describe Marc's ex-wife, and tell what these details suggest about her personality.

_____

_____

5. How is Alice described, and what do these details suggest about her personality?

_____

_____

6. What does Marc reveal as the true reason for the divorce?

_____

Thinking About the Story

7. How does Alice change in her attitude toward Marc and their relationship?

_____

_____

8. Do you think Alice and Marc will live happily ever after? Why or why not?

_____

_____

_____

_____

Name   Class   Date

The Boar Hunt
by José Vasconcelos

Beginning the Story

   Read the story to page 60, through the second paragraph in column 2.

1. List three things the four companions have in common.

_____

2. Give a short, general description of the area the hunters plan to
   explore.

_____

3. List the items the men take along on their expedition.

_____

_____

4. Quote a sentence that shows the wild boar can be a powerful enemy.

_____

_____

5. Find several phrases that demonstrate how formidable the jungle is
   to have as an adversary. Write them in your own words.

_____

_____

6. Describe the mood of the hunters on their first night out.

_____

_____

Continuing the Story

   Continue reading to the end of the story, answering all questions.

7. Which of the five senses does the author appeal to in order to build
   tension in the scene before the boars appear? Give one example.

_____

_____

8. How do the hunters react when they see the first boars appear?
   What do the hunters do?

_____

_____

9. For the first few hours of the "slaughter," the men forget two very
   important facts they had learned about wild boars. What are these
   two facts?

_____

_____

10. As the boars slash furiously at the trunk of the tree in which the
   men hang, what do the hunters wonder about?

_____

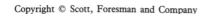

Name   Class   Date

11. Describe the hunters' reactions as the afternoon wanes and the evening comes upon them.

_____

_____

12. Describe the hunters' reactions during the night.

_____

_____

13. What have the boars been doing during the night?

_____

14. In what way is the boars' attack different from the hunters'?

_____

_____

15. How do the hunters perceive the attack by the boars?

_____

_____

16. How does the narrator explain his leap from hammock to tree?

_____

_____

17. What resolution does the survivor make in regard to killing animals?

_____

_____

Thinking About the Story
18. The narrator of this story comes to believe that hunting is "ignoble," or dishonorable. Many people who enjoy hunting wild game would argue with this. What is your feeling on the subject? Write a short essay supporting your ideas.

_____

_____

_____

_____

_____

_____

_____

Name   Class   Date

Life Is Sweet at Kumansenu
by Abioseh Nicol

Beginning the Story

As you read through this story, look for statements that can be understood in more than one way. Read the story until page 67, column 2, where Meji says, "Life is too short."

1. Describe the African village, Kameni.

_____

_____

_____

2. What happened to Bola's first six babies?

_____

3. What does Bola think these babies were?

_____

4. Musa, the village magician, advises Bola to do something to the sixth child. What does he advise, and does she do it?

_____

_____

5. What does Meji look like? How is he dressed? Give a detailed description.

_____

_____

6. What does Meji demand of his mother that so disappoints her during his visit?

_____

7. When Meji says, "They will know soon enough," what do you think he means?

_____

_____

Continuing the Story

Finish reading the story, answering the questions below.

8. Briefly describe the setting for Meji's day with Asi.

_____

9. What do you think Meji really means when he tells his daughter that his watch has stopped at twelve because "the world ends at noon"?

_____

_____

10. Why is Meji able to "speak" to his father in the cemetery through the action of the kola nuts?

_____

Name   Class   Date

11. What statement does Meji make after the graveside ceremony that implies he now has more in common with the dead than with the living?

12. Describe two discoveries made by Bola that evening that cause her to feel uneasy about Meji.

13. What kind of evening is it when Bola and Meji speak for the last time?

14. What facts does Asi contribute as proofs that her father had visited them after Friday noon?

15. What is Musa's explanation for the whole affair?

Thinking About the Story

16. What in the story leads you to disagree with Musa's interpretation of events?

17. Do you think this story could have been set in the middle of a large metropolitan area in the United States? Why or why not?

Name	Class	Date

Home
by Gwendolyn Brooks

Gwendolyn Brooks is best known for her poetry. As you read this short prose sketch, listen for the poetic descriptions in it. Read the story straight through to the end.

1. List the physical objects described in the first paragraph. Include the entire phrase used in the description.

_____

_____

_____

2. Why must the family consider moving?

_____

_____

3. Why do you think Maud Martha holds back her "attack" of Helen's criticisms of the old house?

_____

_____

4. What "mistake" does Maud Martha make in her response to Mama's remark that she has gotten tired of doing the firing?

_____

5. What two senses does Brooks appeal to in the paragraph on page 74, beginning "But she felt . . .," and what is she seeking to emphasize?

_____

_____

6. Find the sentence that first shows you the family will be able to keep their house.

_____

_____

Thinking About the Story
7. Picture a place that has special meaning for you. Write three sentences of *physical* description that suggest why you are fond of it.

_____

_____

_____

_____

_____

_____

_____

Name	Class	Date

Forgiveness in Families
by Alice Munro

Beginning the Story
As you read the story, *listen* very carefully to what the characters say. Listen especially to Cam, since he does not speak very often. Read to page 80, column 1, the point in the story when Cam calls Val and tells her that their mother has "passed out."

1. Read the first paragraph. How would you describe Val's way of communicating?

_____

_____

2. List three things that Val mentions as being representative of the way Cam mishandles situations.

_____

_____

_____

3. After reading Val's review of Cam's life, what do you think she feels are Cam's main flaws?

_____

4. How does Val's mother react to Cam's escapades over the years?

_____

_____

5. Find one paragraph that clearly shows the opposing attitudes Val and her mother have toward Cam. Write it below.

_____

_____

_____

_____

6. What is *your* reaction to Cam when Val describes his current situation at thirty-four years of age?

_____

_____

_____

7. What does Val think brought on their mother's health crisis?

_____

_____

8. Is Cam being true to his character when he calls Val and asks her to come over and help their mother?

_____

Name   Class   Date

Continuing the Story

Continue reading to the end of the story. Note the motives behind Cam's actions and Val's reaction to them.

9. Find at least one sentence that shows Val's outlook on life, one that may help to explain her attitude toward Cam.

_____

_____

10. What is Val's husband Haro's attitude toward his brother-in-law Cam during the crisis?

_____

11. Where had Cam been before he arrives at the hospital? What had he been doing?

_____

12. After his arrival at the hospital, Cam asks a question that indicates he knows exactly what he plans to do for his mother. What is it?

_____

_____

13. When Val's mother takes a sudden turn for the better, Haro says, "You build yourself up ready for something bad to happen and then when it doesn't, it's a queer feeling, you can't feel good right away, it's almost like a disappointment." How does this statement apply to Val's relationship with her brother?

_____

_____

14. Does Cam change after his mother gets well?

_____

Thinking About the Story

15. What does Val learn about herself during the time of her mother's illness and recovery?

_____

_____

Name	Class	Date

Lamb to the Slaughter
by Roald Dahl

Beginning the Story

   Read the title and headnote. Then read to page 90, column 1, where Mary Maloney stands "holding the ridiculous piece of meat tight in both hands."

   1. Give your first impression of Mary Maloney.

_____

   2. How do you know that Mary Maloney is happiest when in her husband's presence?

_____

   3. List the things Mary Maloney loves about her husband. Do they seem very substantial?

_____

_____

   4. What do we learn about Patrick Maloney as he sips his drink?

_____

   5. What do the Maloney's generally do on Thursday night?

_____

   6. Why do you think Mary makes so many attempts to fix food for Patrick when she becomes aware that he is very upset?

_____

   7. What do you think Patrick tells Mary that drives him "further and further away from her with each word"?

_____

   8. How does Mary murder her husband?

_____

Continuing the Story

   Finish reading the story. As you read, compare Mary Maloney in this part of the story to the Mary in the first half.

   9. How does Mary react to what she has done?

_____

   10. Give two possible reasons why Mary goes to the grocery store.

_____

_____

Name   Class   Date

11. Why does Mary pretend that her husband will be waiting at home, tired and hungry?

_____

_____

12. Do you think this sort of pretense is new to Mary?

_____

13. After Mary phones the police station, a total of seven people arrive to investigate Patrick's death. Who are they?

_____

_____

14. What does Jack Noonan believe is the key to finding the murderer?

_____

15. Why does Mary appear to be in a safe position for a murderer?

_____

_____

_____

16. By nine o'clock the men are tired and exasperated. What does Mary do to keep them from asking her any difficult questions and to remind them of their close association with her?

_____

_____

17. Why does Mary Maloney begin to giggle?

_____

Thinking About the Story
18. Do you think Mary will get away with her crime? Explain.

_____

_____

19. This story was once produced for *Alfred Hitchcock Presents* on television. If you were to remake it today, who would you cast in the various roles? Why?

_____

_____

_____

Name   Class   Date

Through the Tunnel
by Doris Lessing

Beginning the Story

Doris Lessing reveals hints about her characters through symbolic details, sometimes obvious, sometimes almost hidden. As you read, ask yourself why certain things have been included: "Why this phrase; why this object?" Read to page 98, column 2, the paragraph in which Jerry gets swimming goggles and runs off "down the steep path to the bay."

1. How do the "wild, rocky bay" and "the crowded beach he knew so well" reflect what is going on in Jerry's life?"

   _____

   _____

2. How does Jerry's mother treat him?

   _____

3. Why is Jerry lonely during his first exploration of the bay?

   _____

   _____

4. List several contrasts between Jerry and the group of boys who come to swim in the bay.

   _____

   _____

5. What are the boys doing as Jerry counts frantically from fifty to one hundred and sixty?

   _____

6. Why does Jerry sit on the diving rock and cry after the boys have left?

   _____

   _____

7. More than once Lessing describes Jerry's mother as a small dot on the beach as Jerry watches her from the bay. Why do you think she is presented in this way?

   _____

   _____

Continuing the Story

Continue reading to the end of the story.

8. Why does Jerry insist he must have goggles?

   _____

   _____

9. What are the two main problems Jerry must solve in order to succeed?

   _____

   _____

10. How does Jerry set about to control his breathing?

_____

_____

11. What physical problem does he develop as he trains?

_____

12. Why does Jerry come to feel that the place where his mother lies
safe in the sun is "not his beach"?

_____

_____

_____

13. When Jerry makes the decision to dive, why is he "trembling with
fear that he would not go"?

_____

_____

14. What technique does Lessing use to emphasize the length of time
Jerry is under water and to increase the suspense of the scene?

_____

15. Why is it "no longer of the least importance to go to the bay"?

_____

_____

Thinking About the Story

16. The wall of rock through which Jerry is determined to swim is very
important in this story. What do you think the rock represents in
life?

_____

_____

_____

_____

17. Have you ever been determined to accomplish some feat or overcome some obstacle? Write about the experience, emphasizing why it
was important to you to succeed.

_____

_____

_____

_____

_____

_____

_____

Name   Class   Date

The Story of the Widow's Son
by Mary Lavin

Beginning the Story

   Read the title and the headnote. Keep in mind the question asked in the headnote as you read. Be aware that there are two endings to this story. Read to where the neighbors are "looking into the fire," on page 107, near the bottom of column 1.

1. What does the author, Mary Lavin, do in the first paragraph to emphasize that what you are reading did not really happen?

_____

_____

2. What are some of the sacrifices the widow makes for her son, Packy?

_____

_____

3. What kind of a boy is Packy?

_____

_____

4. What purpose in the story do you think the neighbor's comments serve as he and the widow wait for Packy's return?

_____

_____

5. What accident happens to Packy?

_____

_____

6. The widow asks many questions to try to piece together an understanding of what has happened. One question, which she continues to repeat for years, hints that she was never able to see things clearly. What is that question?

_____

_____

Continuing the Story

   The writer now offers a new version of the story. Continue reading to the end.

7. What do the neighbors think of Packy?

_____

8. Find a sentence that shows Packy is accustomed to angry outbursts from his mother.

_____

_____

9. Give a reason for the widow's extreme wrath.

_____

_____

Name   Class   Date

10. What happens during her tirade that takes the widow's rebukes down a path even she had not quite expected?

_____

_____

11. How do you know that Packy has noble motives when he leaves home?

_____

12. In the final paragraph, the author reveals her attitude toward making personal choices in life. What does she believe?

_____

_____

_____

Thinking About the Story

13. and 14. In "The Story of the Widow's Son," Mary Lavin writes a fascinating tale of what might have been. Below is the beginning of a story. Imagine that you are the "I" of the story. On a separate piece of paper complete the story. Label this version #13. Next, complete the same story, but this time change the ending. Label this version #14.

I looked out the washed expanse of window into a sheet of rain as I waited to board the 727.

I had saved for over two years for this trip to Europe, and now I was about to be on my

way. As I approached the boarding ramp, someone called my name. There was my sister

Joanie, running to me with fear in her eyes. "What's wrong?" I demanded. "Don't go!" she

yelled. "Something bad will happen if you go! Please don't go!" I

_____

_____

Name   Class   Date

The Chameleon
by Anton Chekhov

Beginning the Story

As you read the story, note where and why the main character, Police Inspector Moronoff, changes sides. Now begin reading to the point at which he commands Grunkin to "Stop arguing!" (page 114, column 2)

1. Describe Police Inspector Moronoff. Give details that indicate his self-image and social status.

_____

_____

_____

2. Describe the neighborhood in which the story takes place. What details hint at the neighborhood's image and social status?

_____

_____

_____

3. As Grunkin explains the biting incident, Moronoff at first takes his side. Why does Moronoff later change his mind?

_____

_____

Continuing the Story

Read the story to the end, answering the questions below.

4. What does Moronoff's statement about the dog, "It's got no coat, it's nothing to look at—just a load of rubbish . . .," reveal about him?

_____

5. When the constable muses that the dog could, in fact, be the General's, what does Moronoff tell him to do?

_____

_____

6. In a normal police investigation, an inspector attempts to reconstruct the facts of the crime. What is the only fact Police Inspector Moronoff is concerned about?

_____

_____

7. Find a short section of the story's dialogue that suggests that the dog, regardless of its owner, was guilty as charged.

_____

_____

Thinking About the Story

8. What commentary on minor public officials in Russia might Chekhov have been making through Moronoff's changeable nature? Would it apply to people in other countries?

_____

_____

Name   Class   Date

Twelve Angry Men: Act One
by Reginald Rose

Beginning Act One

   Take the time now to read the Descriptions of Jurors on page 131.
Since the play begins after the trial has already taken place, these men
will be your only source of information as to what went on in the courtroom. Now begin Act One and continue until the Foreman begins a poll
of the jurors to review the facts (page 136, column 1), saying (to Two),
"I guess you're first."

  1. Why do you think the jurors are identified only by number?

  _____

  _____

  _____

  2. How do you know that Eight is different and alone even before the
     first vote is taken?

  _____

  _____

  3. In a play the writer must insert necessary information into the dia-
     logue without drawing too much attention to the process. List sever-
     al things you learn about the accused as Eight, Three, and the
     others discuss how they voted.

  _____

  _____

  4. How do most of the other jurors react to Eight's statement that they
     owe the boy "a few words. That's all." How are you aware of their
     reactions even before they speak?

  _____

  _____

  5. Why does Twelve propose giving each man a turn to speak his
     mind?

  _____

  _____

Continuing Act One

   Continue reading to the end of Act One.

  6. What important point about the trial-by-jury system in the United
     States does Eight remind Two of as they begin to talk about the
     trial?

  _____

  7. At what time did the murder victim die?

  _____

  8. Who are the witnesses claiming to have heard or seen the boy kill
     his father?

  _____

  _____

Name   Class   Date

9. The people across the hall testified that they heard the boy and his father arguing. What time did that argument take place?

_____

10. What purpose in the play's development do you think the discussion around the table serves?

_____

_____

11. Find a speech by Three that shows he has personal motives for voting guilty. Write a few sentences of that speech.

_____

_____

12. What is Eight's opinion of the lawyer who handled the boy's defense?

_____

_____

13. What important information is revealed about the murder weapon?

_____

_____

14. When Eight calls for another vote, do you think he feels that other jurors may have changed their minds? If so, which one or ones?

_____

_____

Thinking About Act One

15. Choose one of the twelve men in the play and write a paragraph describing the type of father you think he would be. Give details.

_____

_____

_____

_____

_____

_____

_____

_____

Name   Class   Date

Twelve Angry Men: Act Two
by Reginald Rose

Beginning Act Two

  Balloting takes place between acts. The reader/audience is able, therefore, to deliberate just as the jurors do and to make his or her guess regarding who may have changed their votes. Events unfold quickly in Act
Two; read it straight through to the end, answering the questions below.

  1. Who do the other jurors think changed his vote? Who actually did
     write "Not Guilty"?

  _____

  _____

  2. What reason does Nine give for his decision?

  _____

  _____

  3. Why is Four convinced that the woman's testimony is so persuasive?

  _____

  4. What does Three do, as the others discuss the el train, to suggest
     visually how lightly he is taking his responsibilities as a juror?

  _____

  5. What does the discussion about the el train call into question about
     the old man's testimony?

  _____

  _____

  6. When Nine suggests that the old man might have lied, what reason
     for the lie does he give?

  _____

  _____

  7. Why do you think Five changes his vote to not guilty?

  _____

  8. Is it ever proved that the boy *did not* yell "I'm going to kill you!"?
     Explain your answer.

  _____

  _____

  _____

Name _____ Class _____ Date _____

9. Read all the information about the apartment and draw your own
   diagram based on what you learn. Include doorways, stairs, the el
   tracks, the hallway, and the old man's bed.

10. What reason does Three give for not wanting to go through with the
    timed experiment?

_____

11. The jurors tensely watch the re-creation of the old man's walk. Why
    is the result of this experiment so important to their decisions?

_____

12. Do you think Eight deliberately provoked Three into threatening to
    kill him? Defend your answer.

_____

_____

Thinking About Act Two

13. How are the endings of Act One and Act Two similar?

_____

_____

_____

14. If the jurors listed below were to vote again at the end of Act Two,
    how do you think they would vote? Write Guilty or Not guilty after
    each.

FOREMAN _____ FIVE _____ NINE _____
TWO _____ SIX _____ TEN _____
THREE _____ SEVEN _____ ELEVEN _____
FOUR _____ EIGHT _____ TWELVE _____

Name   Class   Date

Twelve Angry Men: Act Three
by Reginald Rose

Beginning Act Three

Between Act One and Act Two time passes as balloting takes place, but between Act Two and Act Three there is no time lapse. The scene is picked up just where we left it. Read Act Three through to the end of the play.

1. The men decide to vote again. Who votes guilty this time around?

2. What reason does Three give for wanting an open ballot? What other unspoken motive might he have?

3. Two has trouble believing that a boy who is five feet eight inches tall could stab downward into the chest of a man six feet two.

   a. What does Three attempt to demonstrate?

   b. What does Five attempt to demonstrate?

   c. Why is Five's demonstration more convincing than Three's?

4. Why does Eleven become angry with Seven?

5. Eight calls for another vote, and the men do so with a show of hands. What is the result?

6. After the latest vote, Ten gives an extended speech in which he lists his "reasons" for voting guilty. What are some of them?

7. Why do you think the woman's evidence, which Four recounts, does not come under discussion until this point in the play?

8. Which juror is most responsible for casting doubt on the woman's testimony?

Name   Class   Date

9. What is brought out about the woman's testimony that makes it suspect?

_____

_____

10. How does the audience find out that Ten has changed his vote to "Not guilty"?

_____

11. What does the way in which Ten agrees there is a reasonable doubt say about how he feels?

_____

12. Nine tells Three that "It takes a great deal of courage to stand alone." In what context was this sentence spoken earlier in the play?

_____

_____

Thinking About the Play
13. Why do you think Three finally voted not guilty?

_____

_____

_____

_____

14. How might the play have ended if Three had not changed his vote?

_____

_____

_____

_____

_____

Name   Class   Date

The Romancers
by Edmond Rostand

Beginning the Play

The play begins with an encounter already in progress between Sylvette and Percinet. Rostand fills in no background, offers no introductions. As you read, pay close attention to the information that is revealed and from whom it comes. Read until page 164, column 2, the point at which Pasquinot orders Sylvette to "Get back in the house—and quickly!"

1. As the play begins, where are Sylvette and Percinet, and what are they doing?

_____

_____

_____

2. Why do you think Sylvette says, "Hush!"

_____

_____

3. Find the speeches of Percinet and Sylvette on page 160 that begin "All right, then let's stop there: . . ." and end ". . . you recite them in your melodious voice. . . ." Rewrite those speeches in plain, contemporary language, including only what is needed to convey meaning.

Percinet: _____

_____

_____

_____

Sylvette: _____

_____

_____

_____

4. In what way do Sylvette and Percinet's parents seem like Romeo and Juliet's?

_____

5. What has Sylvette promised her father?

_____

6. How did the two young lovers meet?

_____

_____

7. Sylvette outlines three "solutions" to their problem. How does Percinet react to them?

_____

_____

8. To what does Bergamin attribute Percinet's strange behavior concerning the wall?

_____

Name   Class   Date

9. What does Bergamin threaten to do to the wall?

_____

_____

10. What does he threaten to do to his son?

_____

_____

Continuing the Play

Continue reading to the end of the play. Pay close attention to Straforel. He has managed to take what Rostand sees as the comic romantic excesses of his day and turn a neat profit.

11. List three things that Bergamin and Pasquinot have in common.

_____

_____

12. What scheme have the two men been hatching over the years?

_____

_____

13. Match the gimmick to some of the abductions offered by Straforel.

 _____ pomp-and-circumstance   **a.** in a sack

 _____ humorous   **b.** in a royal coach

 _____ Venetian   **c.** in masks

 _____ classical   **d.** with musical accompaniment

 _____ gallant   **e.** in a gondola

14. Does the abduction work out as everyone had planned? Explain your answer.

_____

_____

_____

_____

Thinking About the Play

15. Compare Bergamin and Pasquinot to Percinet and Sylvette.

_____

_____

_____

_____

_____

_____

16. The fathers in *The Romancers* believe that by forbidding Sylvette and Percinet to meet they will surely cause them to seek one another out and fall in love. Their plan proves successful. On a separate sheet of paper explain whether you agree that telling children they can't do something can make them want to do it all the more.

Name   Class   Date

Our Town: Act One
by Thornton Wilder

Beginning Act One

Chances are you have never read a play like this one. The Stage Manager never lets you forget that *Our Town* is, in fact, a play. At the same time, he never lets you forget that Grover's Corners is a realistic place. Read only the Stage Manager's speech. Stop just as Joe Crowell, Jr., begins to speak.

1. Draw a map of Grover's Corners. Use your imagination to indicate those details about which the Stage Manager is somewhat vague.

2. What year does the Stage Manager say it is, and what time of day is it as the play begins?

_____

3. The Stage Manager tells us the first auto will come in five years and that Doc Gibbs "died in 1930." What does this information tell us about the Stage Manager's role?

_____

_____

Continuing Act One

Continue reading until Mrs. Gibbs's last speech on page 178, just before the Stage Manager introduces Professor Willard.

4. Dr. Gibbs and Joe Crowell, Jr., have a very simple conversation. At its end, the Stage Manager comments on what you have just heard.

a. _____

What information about Joe Crowell, Jr., do you learn from the Stage Manager? _____

_____

_____

b. How does this information make you feel? Why?

_____

_____

_____

_____

Name   Class   Date

5. As the Webb and Gibbs children prepare for school, their mothers try to keep things running smoothly. List three things Mrs. Gibbs and Mrs. Webb *both* do during this time.

   a. _____ b. _____ c. _____

6. What has Mrs. Gibbs been offered over three hundred dollars for, and what would she like to do with the money?

   _____

   _____

   Continue reading until Emily complains to Mrs. Webb, "Oh, Mama, you're no help at all," on page 182, column 1.

7. Is Professor Willard's information objective or subjective? What do you think is the Stage Manager's purpose in having him give this information?

   _____

   _____

8. The Stage Manager invites the audience to question Editor Webb. Match the people below with the concerns they bring up in their questions.

   Belligerent Man at Back of Auditorium _____   a. culture and love of beauty

   Lady in a Box   _____   b. social injustice and inequality

   Woman in the Balcony   _____   c. liquor consumption

9. George enjoys playing baseball and wants to be a farmer. What does Emily enjoy?

   _____

10. Mrs. Webb tells Emily, "You're pretty enough for all normal purposes." What do you think Mrs. Webb means?

    _____

    _____

   Read to the end of Act One.

11. What does the Stage Manager want to put in the cornerstone of the new bank in addition to the *New York Times*, the *Sentinel*, a Bible, the Constitution, and Shakespeare's plays? What reason does he give for wanting to do so?

    _____

    _____

12. What does Dr. Gibbs speak to his son, George, about?

    _____

13. According to Mrs. Soames, what is "the worst scandal that ever was in this town!"

    _____

Thinking About Act One

14. On a separate piece of paper write a short essay describing what you feel would be the advantages and disadvantages of living in Grover's Corners.

40

Name   Class   Date

Our Town: Act Two
by Thornton Wilder

Beginning Act Two

Three years have passed. As you read, notice similarities and differences between the first two acts. Check your first impressions of George and Emily against what Act Two adds to your knowledge of them. Read the Stage Manager's first speech, then answer the question below.

1. Do couples "marry young" or "marry old" in Grover's Corners? At what approximate age do they marry? Find one sentence to support your answer.

_____

_____

_____

Continuing Act Two

Continue reading until Mr. Webb says ". . . no bridegroom should see his father-in-law on the day of the wedding . . ." (page 192, column 2).

2. In Si Crowell's eyes, what is regrettable about the upcoming wedding of George Gibbs and Emily Webb?

_____

_____

3. As Dr. and Mrs. Gibbs discuss George and Emily's upcoming marriage, Dr. Gibbs reminisces about his own wedding day. What does he recall?

_____

_____

4. Why do you think Mrs. Gibbs makes such an issue of George going out into the rain without his overshoes?

_____

_____

5. What lesson does Mr. Webb want George to learn?

_____

Now read to page 196, to the point where George says, "I'm ready." Pay close attention to those moments when Emily and George speak to one another without hiding their thoughts or feelings.

6. What reason does the Stage Manager give for including the following scene, in which Emily and George first realize "they were meant for one another."

_____

_____

7. What elements of being young and in love does the Stage Manager urge the audience to remember?

_____

_____

8. What reason does Emily give for being mad at George?

_____

_____

9. Why do you think Emily is *really* mad at George?

_____

10. What response does George make to Emily's criticism?

_____

11. What decision does George make about going to State Agriculture College, and why?

_____

_____

_____

_____

Read to the end of Act Two, answering the questions below.

12. The Stage Manager comments that ". . . even at a good wedding there's a lot of confusion way down deep in people's minds. . . ." Who do you think will feel confused in the scene to come, and about what?

_____

_____

_____

_____

13. What is George's reaction to the taunting of the baseball players?

_____

_____

_____

14. What is Emily's initial reaction when she comes on stage in her bridal gown?

_____

_____

Thinking About Act Two
15. What do you think George and Emily's marriage will be like?

_____

_____

_____

_____

_____

_____

Name   Class   Date

Our Town: Act Three
by Thornton Wilder

Beginning Act Three

Nine years have now passed. Read through to the end of the play, being aware that there have been unfortunate changes. Answer the questions below.

1. What is the setting as Act Three begins?

_____

2. What brings Sam Craig back to Grover's Corners?

_____

3. Who has just recently died, and how did it happen?

_____

_____

4. Where did George and Emily get the money to buy the drinking fountain for their stock?

_____

5. Emily decides to go back home. What day does she pick to visit?

_____

6. According to the Stage Manager, are there any people who "realize life while they live it"?

_____

7. Place a check mark next to those things below that Mr. Stimson says are "what it was to be alive."

_____ **a.** laughing at a good joke   _____ **d.** trampling on others' feelings

_____ **b.** moving in a cloud of ignorance   _____ **e.** helping those less fortunate

_____ **c.** holding hands under the stars   _____ **f.** wasting time

8. At the end of the play Emily says, "They don't understand, do they?" Who are "they," and what don't they understand?

_____

_____

_____

_____

Name   Class   Date

Thinking About the Play

9. Each of the characters in the chart below participates in some way in all three acts of the play. In each box, fill in the significant things that character does or what happens to that character in that act.

	Act One	Act Two	Act Three
Dr. Gibbs			
Mrs. Gibbs			
George Gibbs			
Mr. Webb			
Mrs. Webb			
Emily Webb			
Simon Stimson			
Mrs. Soames			
Howie Newsome			
Constable Warren			

Name   Class   Date

Phoebus and Boreas
by La Fontaine / translated by Marianne Moore

Read the entire poem and the footnote, then answer the questions.

1. Who are Phoebus and Boreas?

_____

2. How does the poet, La Fontaine, describe autumn?

_____

3. Is the man in the poem dressed well for the weather?

_____

4. What does the wind propose to do in lines 12-15?

_____

5. Is Boreas's great force confined only to the man? Explain.

_____

6. How does Phoebus win the contest?

_____

The Stone
by Wilfrid Wilson Gibson

Read the poem to the end, then answer the questions below.

1. How did the young man in the poem die?

_____

2. Compare the actions of the "poor fool" (lines 21-29) to the stone that
   killed the young man.

_____

3. What does the woman ask the narrator to do on the fourth night?

_____

4. How do the young woman's grey eyes affect the narrator?

_____

5. What does the woman do as the narrator works?

_____

6. Who does the narrator feel he is working with, and why?

_____

7. What becomes of the young woman?

_____

My Father & The Figtree
by Naomi Shihab Nye

Read the entire poem, answering the questions that follow.

1. To what is the father indifferent?

_____

Name   Class   Date

2. Describe the kind of fig the father is talking about.

_____

3. Why does the mother call her husband a dreamer?

_____

4. What is the song the father chants over the phone?

_____

5. What does the phrase "The last time he moved" tell you about the
   father?

_____

6. Of what are the father's figs "tokens" and "emblems"?

_____

_____

The Fox and the Woodcutter
by Aesop / translated by Denison B. Hull

   Read the entire poem, then answer the questions below.

1. What does the fox ask of the old man cutting wood?

_____

2. How does the woodcutter respond to the fox?

_____

3. What does the woodcutter do when the hunter asks about the fox?

_____

4. Rewrite the poem's moral in your own words.

_____

_____

A Poison Tree
by William Blake

   Read the entire poem. Answer the questions below.

1. In stanza 1, is there a difference between the speaker's anger toward
   his friend and his foe?

_____

_____

2. Is the speaker's occupation with his wrath occasional or constant?
   Explain.

_____

_____

3. Describe the fruit the speaker cultivates with his watery tears, sunny
   smiles, and deceitful wiles.

_____

4. Why do you think the foe steals the apple?

_____

_____

5. What do you think happens to the foe?

_____

Name   Class   Date

I Wandered Lonely as a Cloud
by William Wordsworth

Before reading this lyric poem, read the Writer's Craft on page 234.
Then read the entire poem. Answer the questions that follow.

1. What is the speaker's vantage point as he views the scene in stanza 1?

_____

2. To what does the speaker compare the daffodils in stanza 2, and
   why?

_____

_____

3. Which does the speaker find more gleeful, the waves or the flowers?

_____

4. Look up the word *jocund* in the dictionary if you don't know what it
   means. Check the phrase below that most accurately defines its meaning in this poem.

   _____ to be colorful or brightly painted   _____ funny, joking

   _____ to feel or show cheer   _____ having a great amount

5. What phrase does Wordsworth use in stanza 4 to describe the human
   faculty called *memory*?

_____

6. What is the overall mood of this poem?

_____

The Crazy Woman
by Gwendolyn Brooks

Read the entire poem, then answer the questions below.

1. What do you think is the significance of choosing the months May
   and November?

_____

_____

2. Why doesn't the speaker want to sing a May song?

_____

3. How will her November song sound, according to the speaker?

_____

4. Why do you think the speaker uses the word *little* to describe the
   people who will stare at her?

_____

_____

5. Do you think the speaker is a "crazy woman"?

_____

_____

Name   Class   Date

Hope
by Lisel Mueller

Notice the layout of this poem; it is an example of a visual effect that adds to the meaning of the poem. Read the entire poem, and answer the questions below.

1. In the first sixteen lines, list the verbs the poet uses to help characterize *hope*.

Line 1: _____   Line 9: _____

Line 3: _____   Line 11: _____

Line 4: _____   Line 13: _____

Line 5: _____   Line 15: _____

Line 7: _____

2. How does the layout of the first sixteen lines aid this characterization?

_____

_____

3. In the last eight lines, list the nouns the poet uses to help characterize *hope*.

Line 17: _____   Line 21: _____

Line 19: _____   Line 22: _____

Line 20: _____   Line 24: _____

4. How does the layout of the last eight lines aid this characterization?

_____

_____

New Face
by Alice Walker

1. Rather than worry about love, what has the speaker learned to do?

_____

2. Write the words or phrases in lines 4-15 that suggest a person's intellect is of little value in a love relationship.

_____

_____

3. What seems to be the source of love's mysterious and swift "rush of feelings"?

_____

4. Why do you think "no one else on earth has ever seen" the poet's new face?

_____

_____

Name   Class   Date

To Julia de Burgos
by Julia de Burgos

Here is an interesting poem in which the author wrestles with the two faces she recognizes she wears, one free and artistic, the other socially defined and based in everyday life. Read the entire poem, and answer the questions below.

1. a. Which pronoun identifies the Julia de Burgos who is the "covering"?

_____

    b. Which pronoun identifies the essential Julia?

_____

2. What is the lie referred to in the second stanza?

_____

_____

3. How do you think one's poetry can be thought to give one away?

_____

4. List a few of the many contrasts between the two Julias.

           "I"   "You"

_____   _____

_____   _____

_____   _____

_____   _____

_____   _____

5. What attitude does the poetic Julia have toward Julia the wife?

_____

Don't Ask Me What to Wear
by Sappho

This perfectly wrought poem was written six hundred years before the birth of Christ. Read the entire poem, and answer the questions below.

1. Who is the speaker in this poem?

_____

2. What is the major difference between Cleis and her mother and grandmother?

_____

3. The speaker says, "Don't ask me what to wear," but offers advice anyway. What is her advice?

_____

4. Do you think the speaker exhibits any jealousy? Explain your answer.

_____

_____

Name	Class	Date

The Zoo
by Stevie Smith

Stevie Smith's real name was Florence Margaret Smith, but she used her nickname, "Stevie," on her poems. Read the entire poem before answering the following questions.

1. Where is the lion?

2. Why do you think the same phrase is used in lines 12, 13, and 19?

3. What becomes of the hunter who shouts, "Hallo"?

4. Why does the lion pant?

5. Why does the lion cry?

Ordinance on Lining Up
by Naomi Lazard

Read the entire poem, then answer the questions below.

1. What is one cautioned to do before choosing one of the two lines?

2. Listed below are things associated with the two lines described in the poem. Put an R after those things associated with the right line and an L after those associated with the left line.

moves quickly: _____   one ends as a beggar: _____

is serpentine: _____   moves without hurry: _____

one's beliefs become nonsense: _____

3. Can one change lines after joining one of them? Why or why not?

4. Knowing the eventual destination of the two lines, what do you think is the poet's attitude toward life as revealed in this poem?

5. Which line would you choose? Why?

Name   Class   Date

Improved Farm Land
by Carl Sandburg

Sandburg often uses physical objects and scenes as representatives of an idea. Read the entire poem, then answer the questions below.

1. How large is the "corn belt farm along the Monon"?

_____

2. Indicate below the stages in which the timberland is transformed into farmland.

    a. _____

    b. _____

    c. _____

3. In what sense has the land been "improved"?

_____

_____

4. Why do you think Sandburg characterizes the original landscape as "a great singing family of trees"?

_____

_____

_____

Six Haiku
by Matsuo Bashō and Yosa Buson

Read the Comment about haiku poetry on page 264. Then read the six poems. Answer the questions below after you have read the poems.

1. Find one word in each poem by Matsuo Bashō that suggests the landscape cannot be seen with perfect clarity.

    a. _____

    b. _____

    c. _____

2. List the actions occurring in each of the three poems by Yosa Buson.

    a. _____ and _____

    b. _____ and _____

    c. _____ and _____

3. In the space below, write a haiku that contains your impressions of the scene from your bedroom window. Remember, a haiku is a three-line poem usually containing five syllables in the first line, seven in the second, and five in the third.

_____

_____

_____

Those Winter Sundays
by Robert Hayden

Read the entire poem. Answer the questions below.

1. For what does the father never receive thanks?

2. What kind of job do you suppose the father has?

3. When does the speaker get dressed?

4. How does the speaker of the poem talk to his father?

5. Do you think the speaker would like to thank his father now? Explain your answer.

Harlem
by Langston Hughes

Read the entire poem. Answer the questions below.

1. Look up the word *deferred* in your dictionary. Write its meaning as used in this poem on the line below.

2. List all the distortions the poet suggests a deferred dream may undergo.

3. Which lines indicate that a deferred dream affects the dreamer physically?

4. How do you interpret the last line of the poem?

Afterglow
by Jorge Luis Borges

Read the entire poem slowly. Answer the questions below.

1. What part of the sun's setting bothers the speaker most?

2. What does the sun's last glow do to the plain?

Name   Class   Date

3. How does human fear affect space in the afterglow?

_____

4. To whom is a dreaming sleeper compared?

_____

Sunset
by Oswald Mbuyiseni Mtshali

In this poem, the poet takes a fresh look at the setting sun. Read the entire poem. Then answer the questions below.

1. To what is the sun compared in this poem?

_____

2. What is the sun actually doing when it clicks into the slot?

_____

3. What are the "neon-lights"?

_____

4. In what way has "Time expired" in this poem?

_____

The Naming of Cats
by T. S. Eliot

This poem, one of T. S. Eliot's lighter endeavors, can be heard in the play *Cats*. Read the entire poem. Answer the questions below.

1. List the three different kinds of names a cat must have, according to the poem.

    a. _____   **c.** _____

    b. _____

2. Why does a cat need "a name that's particular"?

_____

3. According to the poem, what is a cat doing when it sits quietly?

_____

For Anne Gregory
by William Butler Yeats

This poem is written as a dialogue between a young man and a young woman. Read it in its entirety, then answer the questions below.

1. In the first stanza a young man tells a young woman why men will love her. What is the reason?

_____

2. What does the woman propose to do in the second stanza? Why?

_____

3. What does the man reply in stanza 3?

_____

Name	Class	Date

The Traveler's Curse After Misdirection
by Robert Graves

The tone of the poem you are about to read is certainly one most people can identify with. The poet is obviously angry with those who have given him misdirection, but his curse is definitely meant to be humorous. Read the entire poem. Then answer the questions below.

1. What is the meaning of the poem's title?

_____

_____

2. What pattern of development does the curse take?

_____

_____

The Fool and the Poet
by Alexander Pope

The creator of this short, humorous verse, Alexander Pope, was one of the great English poets of the 1700s. Read it, then answer the questions below.

1. With what contention, spoken outside of the poem by another person, does the speaker seem to agree?

_____

2. Rewrite the last two lines in your own words.

_____

_____

3. Do you think that Pope really believes what he agrees to in this poem? Why or why not?

_____

_____

4. Pope was one of the great writers of English epigrams, of which this poem is one. An epigram is a short, pointed or witty saying. In the space below try your hand at writing an epigram.

Name   Class   Date

Sonnet 65
by William Shakespeare

This sonnet, while not the oldest poem in this unit, will perhaps seem the least contemporary of them all. It will help your understanding to pay attention to the four questions the speaker poses and then resolves in the final two lines. Read this poem twice through before you attempt to answer any of the following questions.

1. Chart the rhyme scheme for this sonnet (the first four lines are done for you).

    1: a   5: _____   9: _____   13: _____

    2: b   6: _____   10: _____   14: _____

    3: a   7: _____   11: _____

    4: b   8: _____   12: _____

2. According to the poem, which is strongest: brass, stone, earth, sea, or death?

_____

3. To what is beauty's strength compared?

_____

4. How is time able to batter down rocks and steel gates?

_____

5. What is "Time's chest"?

_____

6. In what way can a "strong hand" hold back Time, according to this poem?

_____

_____

7. State in your own words the meaning of the last line.

_____

_____

On the Grasshopper and Cricket
by John Keats

The grasshopper and cricket are related insects. The cricket makes a characteristic "chirping" noise, as do some kinds of grasshoppers. Read the entire sonnet. Answer the questions below.

1. What contrast in setting divides this poem into two parts?

_____

_____

2. Where is the Grasshopper as he sings his song? Where is the Cricket?

_____

3. What similarities can you find in the songs of the Grasshopper and Cricket?

_____

Name   Class   Date

A Round Shape Water Takes Inside the Gourd
by Nguyen Trai / translated by Huynh Sanh

This poem begins with a figurative statement of the theme, continues with an explanation of it, and then expands the theme by giving examples. Read the entire poem, then answer the questions below.

1. What shape does water take when it is *not* inside the gourd?

2. Each of the examples is in two parts, divided by a dash. In the first half of each example, who is responsible for the ultimate result?

3. What do you think this poem reveals about the speaker's view of social classes in society?

4. Below are three aphorisms that also attempt to impart standards of good conduct. Check the one that is most like the poem.

    _____ People in glass houses shouldn't throw stones.

    _____ Lie down with dogs, get up with fleas.

    _____ You can't make a silk purse out of a sow's ear.

In an Iridescent Time
by Ruth Stone

Make sure that you understand the meaning of *iridescent* before you begin to study this poem. Now read the entire poem, listening to its sound as well as thinking about its ideas.

1. Who are the people in the poem, and what are they doing?

2. To which of the five senses do lines 3 and 4 appeal?

3. How does the poet extract the hard work from lines 5 and 6 and transform it into something beautiful?

4. List all of the animal life mentioned in the poem.

5. In line 9, the day is characterized as "soft." Why might that be an unexpected adjective to find at this point in the poem?

6. Why do you think the poet is so careful to mention numbers in the last five lines?

7. What are the two predominant sounds in this poem?

Name   Class   Date

By the Bivouac's Fitful Flame
by Walt Whitman

This poem depicts a scene from the American Civil War (1861-1865).
It can be divided into three parts, signaled by the repetition of the word
procession. Note how the focus of Whitman's poem shifts each time.
Read the entire poem, then answer the questions below.

1. Where is the speaker of this poem?

_____

_____

2. Describe the effect a "fitful flame" would have on its immediate
surroundings.

_____

_____

_____

3. The winding "procession" first mentioned in line 2 is explained more
fully in lines 7-9. What comprises this procession?

_____

4. Why do you think Whitman chose the word *procession* to achieve the
effect of this scene?

_____

_____

_____

5. Below are listed some of the things the speaker notes as he sits by
the campfire. Match the object with how it is perceived by the
speaker.

fields and woods _____   **a.** like a phantom

darkness _____   **b.** seem to be stealthily watching

a figure moving _____   **c.** dim outline

shrubs and trees _____   **d.** lit by spots of fire

6. What kind of thoughts wind through the speaker's mind?

_____

_____

7. Find a phrase near the end of the poem that emphasizes the speaker's
role as observer of the bivouac scene.

_____

Thinking About the Poem
8. List all the *-ing* words Whitman uses in the poem below. What effect
do these words have on the passage of time as created in the poem?

_____

_____

_____

Name   Class   Date

Mrs. Kessler, Hortense Robbins, Samuel Gardner, Dow Kritt, and Cooney Potter
by Edgar Lee Masters

Read the biography and the Comment on page 291. As you read each poem, be sure to spend enough time with its subject to recognize the individuality of the character whose likeness has been taken by the poet. Read the first poem, then answer the questions below.

Mrs. Kessler

1. What major difference do you notice between Mr. and Mrs. Kessler in the first stanza?

_____

_____

2. How does Mrs. Kessler learn so much about the families whose laundry she washes?

_____

3. What does laundry with "rents and patches" tell her about the owners?

_____

4. In what way is life like a laundress?

_____

_____

5. Why do you think the face of a dead person is compared to "something washed and ironed"?

_____

_____

_____

Hortense Robbins

1. Read the entire poem. To what social class did Hortense Robbins belong?

_____

2. In the poem's first seven lines, what aspect of her life does Hortense describe?

_____

_____

3. In the poem's last five lines, where is Hortense?

_____

4. Can you find any irony in this poem? Explain.

_____

_____

_____

Name   Class   Date

Samuel Gardner

1. Read the entire poem. What did Samuel Gardner do for a living?

_____

2. Listed below are various meanings for the word *umbrageous*. Check the one or ones that you think best suits its meaning in this poem.

_____ suspicious   _____ shady   _____ obscure

_____ overshadowing   _____ jealous   _____ apt to take offense

3. What do a tree's roots do with all of the "virtue" they receive from soil, rain, and sun?

_____

_____

4. What relationship does Gardner observe between a tree's branches and its roots?

5. What kind of man would you say Samuel Gardner is (or was)?

_____

_____

Dow Kritt

1. What did Dow Kritt do for a living?

_____

2. What similarities between his elm and Samuel Gardner's does Dow Kritt point out?

_____

3. Why is Dow Kritt's elm dying at the top?

_____

4. What kind of man would you say Dow Kritt is (or was)? Explain.

_____

_____

Cooney Potter

1. Read the entire poem. In what sense was Cooney Potter a self-made man?

_____

_____

2. How did Cooney treat his family?

_____

_____

3. How does Cooney Potter's explanation of his death differ from that of Squire Higbee?

_____

_____

4. Which explanation, if any, seems more likely to you? Answer on a separate sheet of paper.

Name   Class   Date

Oh, When I Was in Love with You, White in the Moon the Long Road Lies, When First My Way to Fair I Took, and An Epitaph
by A. E. Housman

To overintellectualize or overanalyze Housman's poems would be to do them an injustice. Housman hoped his readers would experience his poems, not think about them. Your study in this section should focus on the effect these poems have on you. Read the biography of Housman on page 298. Then read the first poem, answering the questions below.

Oh, When I Was in Love with You
1. What is the cause of the speaker being "clean and brave"?

_____

2. What line in the first stanza tells you that the speaker's way of life while in love was a great change from his past behavior?

_____

3. What is the "fancy" mentioned in line 5?

_____

4. Have you ever changed your behavior to please or impress another? How did it work out?

_____

_____

_____

_____

_____

White in the Moon the Long Road Lies
1. Read the entire poem. Why do you think the speaker notices that the moon "stands blank"?

_____

2. In the second stanza, what contrast is drawn between the speaker and the landscape?

_____

3. Find the line that expresses the notion, as T. S. Eliot has written, "the end is where we start from."

_____

4. What does the speaker feel he must do before returning home again?

_____

5. What does Housman do with individual words and word groups in each stanza to help convey a sense of longing and weariness?

_____

Name   Class   Date

When First My Way to Fair I Took

1. Read the entire poem. How do you know that the young man had a great desire for the goods on display at the fair?

_____

_____

2. Find the line that suggests the speaker is returning to the fair after a considerable passage of time. Why does it suggest this?

_____

_____

_____

3. Rewrite lines 9-12 in your own words.

_____

_____

_____

_____

_____

4. Why do you think the human heart is described as "sore"?

_____

_____

_____

An Epitaph

Be aware that an *epitaph* is a short statement in memory of a dead person, often put on a gravestone or tombstone. Now read the entire poem, addressed to the reader by the grave's occupant. Answer the questions below.

1. What two different meanings for the line "Yet night approaches: better not to stay" are made possible because this poem is an epitaph?

     a. _____

     b. _____

2. While he was alive, how does it appear that the speaker lived his life?

_____

_____

3. How does the speaker look upon death?

_____

_____

4. What do you think the "ancient evil" referred to in the last line is? Why?

_____

_____

_____

Name   Class   Date

Hope Is the Thing with Feathers, The Grass So Little Has to Do, What Mystery Pervades a Well! and A Thought Went Up My Mind To-day
by Emily Dickinson

Emily Dickinson led a private and unpublished life. She had neither special education nor unique experiences; what she had in abundance was imagination and literary talent. Read the biography on page 303, then read the first poem. Answer the questions below.

Hope Is the Thing with Feathers

1. Why do you think Dickinson does not come right out and say in line 1, "Hope is a bird"?

2. Why do you suppose hope's song would be sweetest in a gale?

3. In addition to perching and singing, what else does the "little Bird" do?

4. For all hope does for people, does it ask anything in return?

5. Think of another image a poet might use for hope.

The Grass So Little Has to Do

1. Read the entire poem. Listed below are various things that grass may be said to do. Check only those things grass does in this poem.

   caress the clover _____   stir to the breezes' tunes _____

   hold the sunshine _____   nourish the cows _____

   offer haven to hares _____   bow to everything _____

   dwell in barns _____   entertain small insects _____

2. Find an example of language that projects upon the grass a regal quality.

3. How is the decay that dead grass undergoes different from human decay?

4. Why do you think the speaker in the poem wishes to be hay?

5. This poem is a good example of a literary device that gives human characteristics to nonhuman things. What is that device called?

Name   Class   Date

What Mystery Pervades a Well!
  Read the Comment concerning this poem on page 307. Then read the entire poem. Answer the questions below.

1. What does the speaker see in the well that makes her think of a "neighbor from another world/Residing in a jar"?

_____

_____

2. Why do you think the speaker marvels that the grass growing up around the edge of the well "does not appear afraid"?

_____

_____

3. To what two other things in the poem are the sedge and sea compared?

_____

_____

4. If nature is represented by a haunted house, what do you think the ghost in the poem represents?

_____

_____

5. Does the poet present nature as something we can know and understand? Explain.

_____

_____

_____

_____

A Thought Went Up My Mind To-day
1. Read the entire poem. Has this thought played on the speaker's mind a great deal?

_____

2. Does the speaker know what triggered this thought?

_____

3. Can you think of another title for this poem? Write it below.

_____

4. Have you ever had an experience like the one described in the poem? Write about it on the lines below.

_____

_____

_____

_____

_____

Name   Class   Date

The Road Not Taken, The Exposed Nest, Neither Out Far Nor In Deep, Desert Places, and The Secret Sits
by Robert Frost

Frost's poetry seems so simple, so familiar, so American—and it is. At the same time it carries with it a depth of insight usually reserved for poetry much more abstract and inaccessible. Read the biography on page 309, then read the first poem. Answer the questions below.

The Road Not Taken

1. What season of the year is it?

2. Find the line that states why the speaker chooses one road rather than the other.

3. Did the speaker feel any regret at first for the "road not taken"? How do you know?

4. Do you think the speaker's "sigh" in line 16 is one of sorrow, satisfaction, or resignation? Give your reasons for thinking as you do.

The Exposed Nest

1. Read the entire poem. Describe the chain of events as presented in lines 1-16 of the poem.

2. What right does the speaker's friend wish to return to the young birds?

3. Why does the speaker feel helping the birds is risky?

4. What reason does the speaker give for doing what they did for the birds?

5. What became of the baby birds?

Name _____ Class _____ Date _____

Neither Out Far Nor In Deep

1. Read the entire poem. What common meaning, other than the literal, do you know for the phrase "turn their back on" in line 3?

_____

2. In the poem, does the sea exhibit much action or variety? Explain.

_____

_____

3. Do the "people along the sand" know what they are watching for? How do they feel about this?

_____

_____

Desert Places

1. Read the entire poem. What is the poem's setting?

_____

2. The word *it* is used three times in line 5. Indicate below what each one refers to.

First *it:* _____   Second *it:* _____

Third *it:* _____

3. What does Frost's bending of the word *absent-minded* in line 7 tell you about the speaker?

_____

4. Using your dictionary, explain the double meaning of *benighted* in line 11.

   a. _____

   b. _____

5. In what sense are the speaker's desert places "nearer home"?

_____

The Secret Sits

   Read the poem, thinking about those times when, as a child, you played a game in which one person, sitting in the middle while action went on around him, could not get out without successfully fulfilling some requirement.

1. What do "we" do while "the Secret" sits knowingly?

_____

2. What is the secret?

_____

_____

Name	Class	Date

Half Moon, The Moon Rising, Pause of the Clock, and The Guitar
by Federico García Lorca

Read the biography of García Lorca on page 315. Then slowly read the first poem, two lines at a time. Answer the questions below.

Half Moon

1. Which of the five senses does this poem appeal to?

_____

2. What other art forms appeal only to this sense?

_____

3. How would this poem change if you could hear the scene as well as see it? What sounds might be added?

_____

_____

4. What does the frog see reflected in the water? What does the frog believe this reflection to be?

_____

The Moon Rising

1. Read the poem in four-line units. When the moon rises, bells do not ring and footpaths are impassable. What has the moon done to them?

_____

_____

2. If the sea were to flood the land, what would happen to humans and animals? What, then, does the heart represent in a scene flooded by moonlight?

_____

_____

3. The moon does not give heat and can, at times, take on a blue or green tint along its edge. What does the orange represent that makes it seem out of place in a moonlit environment?

_____

4. What physical characteristics do coins share with the moon? What has the moon done to make the coins sob?

_____

_____

Name   Class   Date

Before reading the next two poems, read the Comment on page 317. This should help you in your reading and interpretation of the poems that you have yet to read.

Pause of the Clock

1. Read the entire poem. The poet is sitting down, perhaps looking up at the night sky. What do the words *backwater, white, ring,* and *stars* suggest to you that he sees?

_____

2. The starlight we see today was generated millions of years ago. Why do you think the stars "collide" with the black numerals?

_____

_____

3. What are the black numerals?

_____

4. How do you think the rhythm of this poem helps communicate a sense of time being stopped or distorted?

_____

_____

The Guitar

Read the poem straight through. Read it again out loud, listening for rhythms. Answer the questions below.

1. The guitar's lament is described as "monotonous." What does the poet do to create a feeling of monotony?

_____

2. Why do you think the person playing the guitar is never mentioned?

_____

3. Some Latin guitars are heart-shaped. What are the "five swords" which pierce the guitar's heart?

_____

4. How many times is some form of the word *weep* used?

_____

5. Find the three phrases or sentences that speak of loss or incompleteness as the emotion behind the lament being played.

_____

_____

_____

_____

Name _____   Class _____   Date _____

The Coronation of Arthur
by Sir Thomas Malory / Translated by Keith Baines

    Before reading this and the following selection, be sure to read pages 327 through 329 in your book. These pages contain a wealth of information about legends, the kinds of people that inhabit them, the philosophies they espouse, and the information they reflect concerning their own time and place. Familiarize yourself with the names and associations of the principal players in the Arthurian legends as they appear on page 329.

    In 1469 or 1470 Sir Thomas Malory finished piecing together eight legends of King Arthur, tales that he called *Le Morte d'Arthur (The Death of Arthur)*. The story you are about to read is one of them. Read the entire selection. Answer the questions below as you read.

1. Identify the role each of the characters listed below plays in Arthur's early life.

   King Uther: _____

   _____

   Queen Igraine: _____

   _____

   Merlin: _____

   _____

   Sir Ector: _____

   _____

2. What must the man who would be the "rightwise" king of Britain do?

   _____

3. What happens on New Year's Day, when Arthur pulls the sword from the stone?

   _____

4. The tournament was repeated more than once. What finally convinces the nobles to recognize Arthur as king?

   _____

from The Hollow Hills
by Mary Stewart

    This version of the same episode in Arthur's life is written from a different point of view. Read the entire selection, answering the questions.

1. Who is telling this account?

   _____

2. Name some of the people in the chapel.

   _____

3. Who did the sword once belong to?

   _____

4. According to the narrator, for whom was the sword made?

   _____

Name   Class   Date

The Lady of the Lake and Excalibur
by Sir Thomas Malory / Translated by Keith Baines

Pay close attention to the role Merlin plays as advisor in this selection as well as in the one that follows it. Merlin is shown to possess prophetic powers, yet Arthur does not always feel compelled to listen to him. Read the selection through to the end, answering the questions below.

1. With whom does Arthur fight, and what is the outcome?

2. What is Excalibur, where does Arthur find it, and who gives it to him?

3. What protection does Excalibur's scabbard offer Arthur, according to Merlin?

4. List Merlin's prophecies as they occur in the story.

    a.

    b.

    c.

    d.

    e.

    f.

Arthur Marries Gwynevere
by Sir Thomas Malory / Translated by Keith Baines

Read the entire selection, answering the questions as you go.

1. When Arthur tells Merlin that Gwynevere has captured his heart, what is the wizard's response?

2. How many knights could be seated at the Round Table?

3. Who was to sit at the Siege Perelous?

4. List the three facets of the knights' Round Table oath.

    a.

    b.

    c.

5. Do you think Arthur and Gwynevere's marriage will be a happy one?

Name   Class   Date

The Tale of Sir Launcelot du Lake
by Sir Thomas Malory / Translated by Keith Baines

Beginning the Selection

Sir Launcelot is to historical Britain what Superman is to contemporary America, an embodiment of the individual and social ideals of the culture taken to their limits. Launcelot's unbroken string of successes in the face of all opposition serve to inspire Britons—the closer they adhere to his ideals, the more successful they will be. Read Malory's tale to page 352, column 1, through the point at which Launcelot finds a pavilion in which to rest "overnight, and continue his search in the morning . . . ." Answer the questions below.

1. At noon, what happens to Sir Launcelot that is uncharacteristic of a vigilant knight?

_____

2. What happens to Sir Lyonel while Sir Launcelot is sleeping?

_____

_____

_____

3. What does Sir Tarquine do with his prisoners once they arrive at his castle?

_____

_____

_____

4. What question does Sir Launcelot's friend, Sir Ector de Marys, ask the forester?

_____

5. What does Sir Tarquine demand of Sir Ector?

_____

6. Four queens come upon Sir Launcelot, and each wants him. What does Morgan le Fay suggest they do?

_____

_____

_____

7. Why do you think Sir Launcelot does not choose one of the four queens in order to save his life?

_____

_____

_____

8. What qualities does King Bagdemagus possess that convince Sir Launcelot to defend him in return for his release from prison?

_____

Name   Class   Date

Continuing the Selection

The next section leads you at a breathless pace through two of Sir Launcelot's many adventures. Continue reading to the end of the story. Answer the questions as you read.

9. List a few of Sir Launcelot's superheroic feats as he fights the King of North Galys and his knights.

_____

_____

_____

_____

10. What reason does Sir Tarquine give for hating Sir Launcelot du Lake?

_____

_____

11. How does Sir Launcelot defeat Sir Tarquine?

_____

_____

_____

12. When does Sir Launcelot return to Camelot?

_____

13. Many of the knights Sir Launcelot had met on his adventures regale the court with tales of Sir Launcelot's exploits. Which two adventures does Sir Launcelot tell himself?

_____

_____

_____

Thinking About the Selection

14. Why do you think those knights defeated by Sir Launcelot are just as willing to tell their stories as those knights who were helped by Sir Launcelot?

_____

_____

_____

_____

_____

_____

_____

_____

_____

_____

Name   Class   Date

from **The Once and Future King**
by T. H. White

Beginning the Selection
Read the entire excerpt, answering the questions below as you read.

1. When asked if he is Sir Lancelot, the reply given is, "I am afraid I am." Do you think Malory's Sir Launcelot would have given such an answer? Why or why not?

_____

_____

2. According to the author, what was the difference between a joust and a tournament?

_____

_____

3. Find a sentence that shows that medieval tournaments and jousts were both serious and artificial, according to White.

_____

4. Do you think White would see much difference between the "merry England" of medieval times and the Northern Ireland of today?

_____

_____

5. In White's retelling of Lancelot's capture and his release by the daughter of King Bagdemagus, how does the author once again exhibit a different view of the knight than did Malory by saying, "He saw at once what he was expected to do."

_____

_____

6. Find two consecutive sentences which show that White considers his work, in one sense, as a commentary on Malory's tale.

_____

_____

Thinking About the Selection
7. Why doesn't Lancelot want the other knights of the Round Table to recognize him?

_____

8. How many opponents does Lancelot defeat in White's telling of the tale?

_____

9. How does White's assessment of the violence of the tournament, which he describes briefly in the final paragraph, differ from Malory's?

_____

_____

Name   Class   Date

The Death of King Arthur
by Sir Thomas Malory / Translated by Keith Baines

Beginning the Selection

Monarchies are simultaneously stable and insecure; all depends on the strength of the royal family. In Arthur's case, there would never be another like him. Read the Comment on page 360, then read the selection to page 364, column 2, where Sir Lucas and Sir Bedivere ride to make a treaty with Sir Modred, offering him "whatever terms he demanded."

1. What differences between medieval times and today made it possible for Sir Modred to usurp the throne as easily as he did?

_____

_____

_____

2. What does Queen Gwynevere do instead of journeying to London for her supposed trousseau?

_____

_____

3. What do the Archbishop of Canterbury's actions regarding Sir Modred tell you about the condition of the church during this time?

_____

_____

_____

4. How is Sir Modred able to win the support of such a large number of people?

_____

_____

5. Find the sentence that clearly identifies the degree of Sir Modred's evil as Malory sees it. Write it in your own words below.

_____

_____

6. According to Malory, why did Arthur's men fight more courageously than Modred's?

_____

7. Why does Sir Gawain feel the need before he dies to be reconciled to Sir Launcelot?

_____

_____

8. What two things does Sir Gawain ask Sir Launcelot to do?

_____

9. How does King Arthur react to the vision he is given in his sleep?

_____

_____

Name   Class   Date

Continuing the Selection

Note how Malory moves between realistic and legendary elements as the account continues. Read to the end of this selection, answering the questions below.

10. What will Modred get in return for signing the truce?

_____

11. Find a sentence suggesting that in spite of all their planning King Arthur and Sir Modred are brought to battle as victims of circumstance. Write the first twelve words of that sentence below.

_____

_____

12. How many men survived the battle? Name them.

_____

13. What reason does King Arthur give for wanting to kill Sir Modred in defiance of the warning in his dream?

_____

14. What is King Arthur's greatest regret surrounding the circumstances of his death?

_____

15. Why do you think Sir Bedivere disobeys King Arthur's command to throw Excalibur into the lake?

_____

_____

16. What happens to the sword when Sir Bedivere finally does throw it into the lake?

_____

_____

17. Where is King Arthur taken in the barge, and why?

_____

18. What do Sir Bedivere and the Archbishop of Canterbury devote themselves to after the king's death?

_____

_____

Thinking About the Selection

19. Why do you think King Arthur's epitaph, "Here lies Arthur, the once and future king," is an appropriate expression for a national legend?

_____

_____

_____

_____

_____

Name   Class   Date

from **Idylls of the King**
by Alfred, Lord Tennyson

Beginning the Poem
Read the entire poem, then answer the questions below.

1. What distinguishes the "true old times" from those that follow?

_____

_____

2. What did the Round Table symbolize?

_____

3. Find the lines in which Tennyson suggests that it is a good thing for the world of Arthur to pass away. Write them below.

_____

_____

_____

4. How does Tennyson distinguish men from animals?

_____

5. Why do you think King Arthur doubts that he will be taken to Avilion (Avalon)?

_____

6. How does Tennyson describe Avilion?

_____

_____

7. What is Sir Bedivere doing as the barge sails away?

_____

Thinking About the Poem
8. Why do you think Tennyson has King Arthur's barge move toward the dawn, rather than north, south, or west?

_____

_____

_____

_____

Name   Class   Date

The Necklace
by Guy de Maupassant

Beginning the Story

   Read the title and headnote and look at the picture on page 381. Then read the first part of the story and all footnotes. Stop at the space in column 1, page 383.

1. Find the phrase that indicates the woman is not happy in her marriage. Write it below.

   _____

   _____

   _____

2. According to the narrator, what characteristics of womanhood are able to overcome a lack of money, education, or social status?

   _____

   _____

3. In your own words, how does the young woman compensate for the modest way of life she lives?

   _____

   _____

4. What two things does the woman love?

   _____

5. How does she react to the invitation she receives? Why?

   _____

   _____

6. What does *Mme.* Loisel's husband suggest she wear in place of jewelry?

   _____

7. Below is a list of the jewelry *Mme.* Loisel is invited to choose from by her friend *Madam* Forestier. Check the one item she asks to borrow.

   a collar of pearls _____   a necklace of diamonds _____

   a ruby bracelet _____   a Venetian cross of gold and jewels _____

Continuing the Story

   Continue reading the rest of the story, answering the questions below.

8. Find at least one sentence which shows that, at the ball, *Mme.* Loisel was in fact charming and beautiful, that her self-image was not completely vain imagination.

   _____

   _____

9. Why does *Mme.* Loisel cry out when she looks at herself in the mirror?

   _____

Name   Class   Date

10. List three things *M*. Loisel does to find the lost necklace. Is he
successful?

_____

_____

_____

11. What does Loisel then tell his wife she must do?

_____

_____

12. How is Loisel able to replace the lost necklace?

_____

_____

13. How does *Mme*. Forestier react to Matilda when she returns the
necklace?

_____

14. Find one sentence that reveals Matilda had been living in a situation
that was not quite as impoverished as her opinion of it.

_____

15. How long does it take them to pay off the debt?

_____

16. How do the years of hard work change Matilda?

_____

_____

_____

17. What does *Mme*. Loisel learn about the necklace when she speaks
with *Mme*. Forestier on the Champs Élysées?

_____

_____

Thinking About the Story

18. What do you think Matilda's reaction is to learning that she had al-
tered the complete course of her life unnecessarily?

_____

_____

_____

_____

_____

_____

Name	Class	Date

The Interlopers
by Saki

Beginning the Story

Read the title and headnote and look at the picture. Then read the first part of the story and all footnotes. Pay close attention to Saki's detailed settings, which manipulate mood. Stop at the end of the paragraph on page 390, column 2, that begins "Both men spoke with the bitterness of possible defeat before them. . . ."

1. Why is Ulrich von Gradwitz out in the forest on a winter night?

2. How valuable is the disputed territory that Gradwitz guards so jealously?

3. When the story begins, how long has the feud lasted?

4. Name the man Ulrich detests and would like to see come to harm.

5. What has kept the feud from ending?

6. Find a sentence in the third paragraph that alerts the reader to the possibility that all is not well in the forest.

7. Does Ulrich have any idea as to the cause of the disturbance? Explain.

8. Do you think it is realistic that Ulrich and Georg meet face to face as they do? Why or why not?

9. What happens as the men stand facing one another?

10. After they realize their predicament, what attitude does each man at first have toward his enemy?

Name   Class   Date

Continuing the Story

Continue reading to the end of the story, answering the questions below.

11. Ulrich manages to reach his wine flask and take a draft. What does he do next?

_____

12. How does Georg respond to Ulrich's offer?

_____
_____

13. What does Ulrich call Georg, signaling that he no longer wishes to continue their feud? What proposition does he offer?

_____
_____
_____

14. What is Georg's reaction?

_____

15. What benefit to others does Georg foresee their newfound friendship having?

_____

16. For the first time in their lives, the two men do something together. What is it?

_____

17. Georg sees figures coming toward them. How many does he think there are?

_____

18. Whose men do the figures turn out to be?

_____

Thinking About the Story

19. Would this story be as effective if the men were rescued? Why or why not?

_____
_____
_____
_____
_____
_____
_____

Name   Class   Date

The Man from Kabul
by Rabindranath Tagore

Beginning the Story

Read the title and headnote and look at the pictures on pages 395 and 397. Then read the first part of the story and all footnotes. Stop at the end of column 2 on page 396. Answer the questions below.

1. How old is Mini?

_____

2. In the first six paragraphs, find several words that describe Mini as an active child.

_____

3. What is the narrator's profession?

_____

4. Describe the Kabuliwallah.

_____

_____

5. What does Mini fear the Kabuliwallah has in his bag?

_____

6. What do the narrator and the Kabuliwallah discuss?

_____

7. How does Mini behave during her first meeting with the Kabuliwallah?

_____

_____

8. One day the narrator is surprised to find that his daughter and the Kabuliwallah have become friends. In what way is the Great Kabuliwallah like Mini's father?

_____

9. Why do you think the narrator finds Mini's conversations with the Kabuliwallah "fascinating"?

_____

_____

10. Define the two different meanings of "father-in-law's house" as discussed in the story.

_____

_____

11. The presence of the Kabuliwallah excites the narrator's imagination. What simile does the author use to describe the narrator's existence as compared to the wanderings of the turbaned visitor?

_____

12. How does Mini's mother feel about her daughter's unusual friend?

_____

Name   Class   Date

Continuing the Story
  Continue reading the story, answering the questions below.

13. Why is Rahman, the Kabuliwallah, arrested?

_____

_____

14. What does Mini ask Rahman before he is taken away, and how does
  he respond?

_____

_____

15. On the day of the evening Mini is to be married, the Kabuliwallah
  comes to the house. What does he ask of the father, and what response is he given?

_____

_____

16. What is on the piece of paper Rahman shows the narrator?

_____

_____

17. When Mini finally appears before him, what does Rahman, in his
  turn, ask her, and how does she respond?

_____

_____

18. For what two reasons does Rahman's meeting with Mini as a woman
  sadden him?

_____

_____

_____

Thinking About the Story

19. Why do you think this story was told from the father's point of
  view rather than from Mini's or Rahman's?

_____

_____

_____

_____

_____

_____

_____

_____

_____

_____

Name	Class	Date

A Letter to God
by Gregorio López y Fuentes

Beginning the Story

In order to read this story properly, remember that Lencho is a simple farmer, but he is not stupid. It is faith, not foolishness, which directs his actions. Read the entire story. Then answer the questions below.

1. Describe the place where Lencho lives.

_____

_____

2. Does Lencho expect a fruitful harvest this season?

_____

3. Is Lencho afraid that lack of rain will ruin his crops? Why?

_____

4. To what does Lencho compare the drops of rain that fall?

_____

5. Why is it fitting that Lencho makes this particular comparison?

_____

6. To what are the hailstones compared?

_____

7. In what sense are the last two hailstone comparisons ironic?

_____

_____

8. Is Lencho as confident the hail will stop as he was that the rain would begin? How do you know?

_____

9. What is Lencho's economic condition after the hailstorm?

_____

10. What does the family feel is their one source of hope?

_____

11. What does Lencho decide to do about his situation?

_____

12. What does Lencho ask for?

_____

Name   Class   Date

13. How do the two men who see the address on Lencho's letter react to it?

_____

_____

14. After reading the letter, what does the postmaster decide to do?

_____

_____

15. Is Lencho surprised to receive a letter from God? Explain his reaction.

_____

_____

16. What is ironic about Lencho's second letter to God?

_____

_____

_____

Thinking About the Story

17. Why do you think Lencho mails a letter to God, rather than praying?

_____

_____

_____

_____

18. What does the postmaster's willingness to give Lencho less money than he requested tell you about the postmaster's view of God?

_____

_____

_____

_____

19. Why does Lencho make the assumption that the post office employees stole forty pesos?

_____

_____

_____

_____

Name	Class	Date

The Sentimentality of William Tavener
by Willa Cather

Beginning the Story

There is one key concept to keep in mind as you read this story, and that is *sentimentality*. To be sentimental, in the best sense, means to openly show one's emotions to another. Read the first part of the story. Stop after the third paragraph on page 409, column 1, which begins "You've been short of hands all summer . . ."

1. What kind of woman is Hester Tavener?

_____

_____

_____

_____

2. What kind of man is William Tavener?

_____

_____

_____

_____

3. How does William react to Hester's "agitation?"

_____

_____

4. To what does the author, Willa Cather, compare William's indifference toward changes in his family's moods?

_____

_____

5. How long does Hester hesitate before voicing her concerns?

_____

6. What is it that Hester is upset about?

_____

7. What arguments does Hester offer for allowing the boys to do what they want to do?

_____

_____

8. Look up the word *greenhorn* if you don't know what it means. Why do you think Hester is worried about the boys growing up to be greenhorns?

_____

_____

Name   Class   Date

Continuing the Story

Continue reading to the end of the story, answering the questions below.

9. What attractions does Hester remember seeing at the circus she attended with her father?

_____

_____

10. What correction to Hester's reminiscences does William offer?

_____

_____

11. How did William Tavener happen to go to the circus?

_____

_____

12. When does William find himself thinking about the clown of long ago?

_____

13. How does Cather give the reader a vivid impression that Hester finds William's story of utmost interest?

_____

_____

14. What common experiences had caused the Taveners' relationship to become like that of "landlord and tenant"?

_____

_____

15. What does sharing their recollections of the circus do to change the Taveners' relationship?

_____

_____

16. What other things do the two go on to discuss?

_____

_____

17. What does William Tavener do when the clock strikes ten?

_____

_____

18. After William has fallen asleep, what does Hester do?

_____

_____

Thinking About the Story

19. In what way have Hester's sons "lost a powerful ally"?

_____

_____

_____

Name   Class   Date

The Rocking-Horse Winner
by D. H. Lawrence

Beginning the Story

Read the title and headnote on page 413. Then read the beginning of the story, to the place where Paul rides furiously to "where there is luck" (page 415, column 1).

1. What does the beautiful woman of the story lack?

_____

2. What is it that the woman and her children know that no one else knows?

_____

3. How do they know it?

_____

4. What kind of life do these people live?

_____

_____

5. What unspoken phrase do the children hear all the time?

_____

6. When Paul asks his mother why they are poor, what does she answer?

_____

7. Paul tells his mother he is lucky. When she asks why, what does he reply?

_____

8. What does Paul command his horse to do?

_____

Continuing the Story

Continue reading until Paul begs Uncle Oscar not to tell his mother what is going on. Uncle Oscar agrees that they can "manage it without her knowing" (page 419, column 2).

9. How does the author, D. H. Lawrence, describe Bassett regarding his knowledge of horse racing?

_____

10. What horse does Paul tell his Uncle Oscar to bet on in the Lincoln?

_____

11. How much money does Paul plan to bet?

_____

12. How much money does Paul tell his uncle he has made betting on horse races?

_____

13. To what does Bassett attribute Paul's uncanny ability to pick winning horses?

_____

Name   Class   Date

14. When Uncle Oscar asks, "... what makes you sure, sonny?" what does Paul reply?

_____

15. What does Paul hope will happen if he is lucky?

_____

Read the story to the end, answering the questions below.

16. What scheme do Paul and his uncle devise to give his mother five thousand pounds without her knowing where it came from?

_____

_____

_____

17. Why is Paul's mother dissatisfied with her job at the drapers?

_____

_____

18. How does Paul's mother use the five thousand pounds? Do you think she uses it well?

_____

_____

19. What happens to the voices in the house?

_____

20. What is the boy's "secret of secrets"?

_____

21. What is the violent, powerful, hushed sound Paul's mother hears as she enters the house after returning from the party?

_____

22. What happens to Paul after he screams, "It's Malabar!"

_____

23. What phrase does Uncle Oscar repeat several times in the final paragraph that suggests Paul's "luck" may have had a source other than God?

_____

Thinking About the Story

24. Why do you think Paul was compelled to ride his rocking-horse in order to "take him to where there was luck"?

_____

_____

_____

_____

_____

Name   Class   Date

The Needle
by Isaac Bashevis Singer

Beginning the Story

You are about to read a marvelous story based on a folk tale. It takes traditions, superstitions, facts, and legends common to a community and mixes them together in an imaginative way. Read to the point at which Esther Rosa announces, "You will be my Benze's wife, God willing" (page 430, column 2).

1. How did marriages come about in the narrator's day?

2. What would Reitze Leah do when searching for a bride for one of her sons?

3. What does the narrator claim is the primary factor in entering into a *successful* marriage?

4. Describe Esther Rosa.

5. Describe Esther Rosa's son, Ben Zion.

6. What does Esther Rosa spend most of her time doing? Is she successful at it?

7. What does she want most in the girl who will be Benze's wife?

8. What practical talents does Esther Rosa possess?

9. To what town do the narrator, Zeldele, and Esther Rosa travel in search of a bride?

10. What physical characteristic of the salesgirl in Berish Lubiner's dry-goods store acts as a symbol of her personality?

Name _____ Class _____ Date _____

11. What physical characteristic of the salesgirl in Reb Zelig Izbitzer's dry-goods store acts as a symbol of her personality?

_____

12. What does the salesgirl reply when Esther Rosa asks her why she is going to such trouble for such a small sale?

_____

_____

_____

13. What does Esther Rosa tell the salesgirl she is to become?

_____

Continuing the Story

Continue reading to the end of the story, answering the questions below.

14. Listed below are some of the misfortunes that befall Itte Berish and a few that do not. Check only those things that actually happen to her in the story.

    _____ she falls and breaks a leg   _____ her sisters won't speak to her

    _____ she becomes ill   _____ untrue stories are told about her

    _____ she cries night and day   _____ the store begins to fail

    _____ she acquires a bad name   _____ she cannot find a husband

15. List two additional tragedies that happen to Itte.

_____

16. Why do the salesgirls of Zamosc become so polite?

_____

_____

17. What is the narrator's view of personal effort in determining the outcome of an individual's affairs?

_____

_____

_____

Thinking About the Story

18. What piece of information about each of the two salesgirls is withheld for a time by the author? Why do you think the author does so?

_____

_____

_____

_____

Name   Class   Date

The Rat Trap
by Selma Lagerlöf

Beginning the Story

Here is a story in which the main character's view of others is influenced to a high degree by the way life has treated him. Read the first half of the story. Stop at page 437, column 2, where the vagabond thinks, "Now I am sitting in the trap and will never get out of it."

1. What does the man do to try and make a living?

_____

2. What thought occurs to the vagabond as he trudges along the road?

_____

3. How does this thought make him feel?

_____

_____

4. How is the vagabond treated by the man in the small gray cottage?

_____

_____

5. After the vagabond says good-bye and the crofter goes off to milk his cow, what does the vagabond do?

_____

_____

6. How does the vagabond feel about what he has just done?

_____

7. The vagabond thinks the money he has stolen is "a bait" by which he has been caught. What becomes his prison?

_____

8. What does the vagabond hear, and what does he do?

_____

9. Describe the vagabond from the blacksmiths' point of view.

_____

_____

10. How does the master blacksmith treat the vagabond?

_____

11. Why does the vagabond not reveal the ironmaster's mistake in thinking he is Nils Olof?

_____

12. What is the vagabond's initial reaction to the ironmaster's invitation to come home with him?

_____

13. Why does Edla Willmansson come to the forge?

_____

Name   Class   Date

14. What does Edla realize about the vagabond?

_____

15. Find a sentence which shows that the vagabond considers his current predicament a direct result of his burglary.

_____

_____

Continuing the Story

Continue reading to the end of the story.

16. What does the ironmaster realize once the vagabond is clean and well-dressed?

_____

17. Why does Edla intercede for the vagabond?

_____

_____

18. How does the vagabond pass most of Christmas Eve?

_____

19. How does the vagabond respond to Edla's offer to spend next Christmas Eve with them?

_____

20. What does Edla learn the next day at church?

_____

21. What is in the package the visitor has left for Edla Willmansson?

_____

_____

Thinking About the Story

22. Why do you think the vagabond signed himself *Captain von Ståhle?*

_____

_____

_____

_____

_____

_____

_____

_____

_____

_____

Name	Class	Date

Enemies
by Nadine Gordimer

Beginning the Story

The two women in this story are opposites in many ways. One is withdrawn, proper, seeking to remain alone. The other is talkative, somewhat uncouth, and in search of company. The author provides a great deal of information about each woman; try not to overlook any of it. Read the beginning of the story. Stop at the break in column 2, page 446. Answer the questions below.

1. Mrs. Clara Hansen is described as "withdrawn as a castle." Name some characteristics of a castle which make this an appropriate simile.

_____

_____

2. List a few of the many things Alfred does to assure Mrs. Hansen of a comfortable journey.

_____

_____

3. Is Alfred portrayed as a disloyal employee attempting to fool Mrs. Hansen in some way? Explain.

_____

_____

4. At this point in the story, with Alfred standing outside the train and Mrs. Hansen looking out from within, who do you think the rest of the story will be about—Alfred or Mrs. Hansen? Why?

_____

_____

5. Find the simile that describes the appearance of the old woman next door.

_____

_____

6. In the first paragraph on page 446, Mrs. Hansen thinks about two enemies. Who are they?

_____

7. How old is Clara Hansen?

_____

8. Does Mrs. Hansen make a distinction between being *alone* and being *lonely?*

_____

_____

9. Why does Mrs. Hansen take her dinner in the dining car?

_____

_____

Name   Class   Date

Continuing the Story

Continue reading to the end of the story, answering the questions below.

10. When the other woman joins Mrs. Hansen for dinner, how does Clara treat her?

11. Why does Clara Hansen believe that "good teeth as well as bad aches and pains" should be kept to oneself?

12. How much of the year does Clara Hansen spend traveling?

13. Do both women have families? Explain.

14. What does Mrs. Hansen hear coming from the compartment next to hers?

15. What does Mrs. Hansen assume is the cause of what she hears?

16. What happened to the woman in the compartment next door?

17. To whom does Clara Hansen send a telegram, and what does it say?

Thinking About the Story

18. Mrs. Hansen thinks of herself in terms of her "real" self and her "Old Fool" self. How do the two differ, which does she fight to suppress, and why?

19. Why does Clara Hansen choose Alfred as the recipient of her telegram, and what do you think his reaction will be?

Name   Class   Date

Action Will Be Taken
by Heinrich Böll

Beginning the Story

Unlike the other stories in this unit, this one is humorous. As you
read the story, go ahead and laugh; art allows it. Read to page 454, column 2, where the narrator says, "I felt something like tenderness for
him, . . ."

1. Why does the narrator need to find work?

_____

2. Why do you think he is averse to well-lit buildings and rooms, and
   suspicious of cheerful coffee shops?

_____

3. Why does the narrator drink his orange juice, leave the coffee and
   egg, and pace the coffee shop?

_____

_____

4. What phrase does the narrator use more than once to suggest that he
   is making a conscious effort to look eager for work?

_____

5. At left below are the three questions the narrator was given on the
   questionnaire. To the right are his three answers. Match the answer
   he gave to the question asked.

   _____ *"Do you consider it right for a*   a. "There have to be nine before I am working
   human to possess only two arms, two legs,   to capacity."
   and two ears?"

   _____ *"How many telephones can you*   b. "I no longer acknowledge the term. . . ."
   handle at one time?"

   _____ *"How do you spend your free*   c. "Human beings are very poorly equipped."
   time?"

6. What does the narrator have to say about "vigorous personalities"
   who are always talking about their lives?

_____

_____

7. Below are three of the energetic people the narrator encounters at
   Wunsiedel's factory. List one or two things each does that illustrate
   his or her fanatical need for activity.

   Broschek: _____

_____

   Wunsiedel's secretary: _____

_____

   Wunsiedel: _____

_____

8. After two weeks on the job, how many telephones does the narrator
   now have?

_____

Name   Class   Date

9. What happens to Wunsiedel?

_____

10. What preposterous things is Broschek doing when the narrator goes
to his office to tell him about Wunsiedel?

_____

_____

_____

Continuing the Story

Read to the end of the story, answering the questions below.

11. What action is taken concerning Wunsiedel?

_____

12. Why is the narrator chosen to follow the coffin carrying a wreath?

_____

13. Why does the narrator quit his job?

_____

14. What reason does he give Broschek for leaving?

_____

15. Why does the narrator feel an obligation to visit Wunsiedel's grave?

_____

16. What did the narrator fail to find out about Wunsiedel's factory?

_____

Thinking About the Story

17. There is probably no way of knowing why the narrator concludes
that it was soap Wunsiedel's factory was producing. Take a guess as
to why he thinks it was soap, anyway.

_____

_____

_____

18. What do you think is the significance of the fact that Wunsiedel's
ringing call, "Action will be taken!" is cast in the _passive_ voice?

_____

_____

_____

Name	Class	Date

Miss Brill
by Katherine Mansfield

Beginning the Story

In order to fully appreciate this story, you must become Miss Brill's companion, observing what she observes, hearing what she hears. Test her reading of events against your own. Read the first part of the story. Stop on page 460, column 2, after the bands plays "Tum-tum-tum tiddle-um!"

1. What level of social class does Miss Brill project into the weather she is experiencing today? List several phrases to support your answer.

_____

_____

2. What is the setting of the story?

_____

3. How does Miss Brill treat the fur she is wearing?

_____

_____

4. According to Miss Brill, why does the band play differently once "the Season" begins?

_____

_____

5. What simile does the author, Katherine Mansfield, use to describe the conductor of the band?

_____

6. What is it that Miss Brill looks forward to as she sits in her "special" seat?

_____

_____

7. What level of attention does Miss Brill give to the conversations going on around her?

_____

_____

8. What does Miss Brill do as she sits in the park?

_____

9. Listed at left below are some of the things Miss Brill sees as she sits watching the crowd. At right are phrases the author uses to describe them. Draw lines to match the description to the thing described.

little girls	like a young hen
little boys	little French dolls
little children	with big bows under their chins
high-stepping mother	swooping and laughing

Name   Class   Date

10. What does Miss Brill think of the people sitting on chairs and benches?

_____

_____

Continuing the Story

Read to the end of the story, answering the questions below.

11. How does the author make you, the reader, aware that Miss Brill views these concerts more as theatrical events?

_____

_____

_____

12. Why does the band seem to Miss Brill to be playing more softly, the drum beating "The Brute! The Brute!" over and over?

_____

_____

13. What does Miss Brill come to realize about her role in the play she is watching?

_____

14. How does the author describe the way Miss Brill envisions the newspaper she reads to the elderly invalid?

_____

15. As she listens to the band begin to play again, what does it seem to Miss Brill everyone will do?

_____

16. Miss Brill prepares herself to enjoy a "scene" between a "hero and heroine, of course, just arrived from his father's yacht." Do they deliver the expected dialogue? What makes their dialogue so unusual?

_____

_____

_____

17. What does Miss Brill forsake doing that she usually does on Sundays after the concert?

_____

Thinking About the Story

18. Do you think that Miss Brill will continue to wear her fur piece? Support your answer.

_____

_____

_____

19. Find a spot in your home or neighborhood where you can sit and observe what is going on around you. On a separate piece of paper, write about what you see and hear.

Name   Class   Date

Tuesday Siesta
by Gabriel García Márquez

Beginning the Story

This story is a translation from the original Spanish. Remember that the characters are from a non-English-speaking culture. Do not unconsciously place the events in the United States. Read the story to page 468, the bottom of column 1.

1. Describe the two people traveling by train in the third-class car.

_____

_____

_____

2. Look up the word *severe* in your dictionary. Why is this an appropriate way of describing their mourning clothes?

_____

_____

3. What is it like inside the car?

_____

_____

4. As the two eat, the train passes through a town. What is happening in the town plaza?

_____

5. Write three of the things the woman instructs her daughter to do (or avoid doing).

_____

_____

_____

6. What day of the week and month of the year is it?

_____

7. What does the description of the town as mother and daughter arrive tell you about its way of life?

_____

_____

8. When do the stores, offices, and school close and reopen?

_____

9. Where do the woman and girl go in the town?

_____

10. The woman is told to come back after three. What does she reply?

_____

Name _____ Class _____ Date _____

Continuing the Story

Read the rest of the story, answering the questions below.

11. What does the woman want from the priest, and why?

_____

_____

12. Who killed Carlos Centeno, and how?

_____

_____

13. What were the intruder's last words?

_____

14. How does the mother attempt to prove to the priest that her son
was not a bad man?

_____

_____

_____

15. Why does the priest tell the woman to "Wait until the sun goes
down"?

_____

_____

16. What do the woman and girl do?

_____

_____

Thinking About the Story

17. Why do you think the mother and daughter choose to leave the
priest's house by the front door even though they have been warned
that many of the town's residents have come outside to watch them
pass?

_____

_____

_____

_____

_____

_____

_____

_____

Name   Class   Date

The Demon Lover
by Elizabeth Bowen

Beginning the Story

Throughout this story you will sense a tension between natural, everyday experiences and a supernatural aura that envelops them. Read to the
break in column 1, page 474, answering the questions as you read.

1. List several details from the first paragraph that help to create a
   mood of mystery.

   _____   _____

   _____   _____

   _____   _____

2. List two of the "traces" of her old way of life that Mrs. Drover sees
   in the house and finds puzzling.

   _____

   _____

   _____

3. Why are there cracks in the interior of the house?

   _____

4. What does Mrs. Drover find on the hall table?

   _____

5. Why is it strange that she should find it there?

   _____

6. Where does Mrs. Drover decide to take it?

   _____

7. Who do you think the letter is from?

   _____

8. When Mrs. Drover looks into the mirror, what does she see?

   _____

   _____

   _____

Continuing the Story

The next section of the story deals with Kathleen Drover's past. Try
to form a clear picture of the relationship between Kathleen and the
young man. Now read to page 474, the bottom of column 2, where Mrs.
Drover dismisses the idea that her movements "were still watched."

9. What did the young Kathleen, now Mrs. Drover, have as a memen-
   to of her relationship with her soldier?

   _____

Name _____ Class _____ Date _____

10. Describe Kathleen's fiancé.

_____

_____

_____

11. What does he tell her she need only do?

_____

12. In what way has Kathleen "plighted a . . . sinister troth"?

_____

_____

13. When her fiancé does not return, does Kathleen have other beaus?

_____

_____

Continue reading to the end of the story.

14. What metaphor is used to describe Mrs. Drover's London home as it is now?

_____

_____

15. Mrs. Drover cannot determine how the letter got into her locked house. She locks the door to her room and begins putting parcels together. What does she plan to do when the parcels are wrapped?

_____

16. What lapse in Mrs. Drover's memory of her fiancé scares her above all else?

_____

_____

17. When Mrs. Drover leaves the house, where does she go?

_____

18. What does she see at the corner of the square?

_____

19. What does Mrs. Drover do when the taxi driver turns and faces her?

_____

Thinking About the Story

20. Who is driving the taxi, and where do you think he is taking his passenger?

_____

_____

_____

_____

Name   Class   Date

The Masque of the Red Death
by Edgar Allan Poe

Beginning the Story

The central concept for this story is that of the *masque*. In past centuries it meant much more than just a masquerade or costume party. The masque was a very specific type of dramatic event in which, with extravagant costumes, music, and broad physical action similar to mime, an allegorical or legendary story would be presented. Read the Comment on page 484 for insight into the story you are about to read. Then read to the bottom of the first column on page 482.

1. Listed below are a number of symptoms associated with illnesses. Check only those that the narrator attributes to the "Red Death."

   heart palpitations _____   sharp pains _____   dissolution _____

   dizziness _____   bleeding _____   chronic cough _____

   paralysis _____   slow onset _____   tremors _____

   nausea _____   sudden onset _____   scarlet stains _____

2. How are victims of the disease treated by others?

   _____

   _____

3. Why do Prince Prospero and his band of courtiers retire to the abbey and bolt its gates?

   _____

4. What do they believe it is "folly" to do?

   _____

5. How much time passes before Prince Prospero holds his masked ball?

   _____

6. What is to be found in the middle of each wall of the seven rooms of Prince Prospero's imperial suite, and what do they look like?

   _____

   _____

7. What made the effect of the last of the seven suites different from all the others?

   _____

8. What illuminates the rooms?

   _____

9. Why do so few of Prospero's guests chose to enter the seventh room?

   _____

   _____

10. Find a phrase in column 2 of page 480 that may serve to remind readers that Prospero's attempt to stop time and death are futile.

   _____

   _____

Name   Class   Date

11. List some of the words Poe uses to describe the masqueraders.

_____

_____

12. More than once Poe describes the guests' movements as "writhing."
If you are unsure of its meaning, look up *writhe* in your dictionary.
What does this word tell you about the guests?

_____

_____

_____

Continuing the Story

Continue reading to the end of the story, answering the questions.

13. Why are the guests so upset by the tall, gaunt masquerader?

_____

14. How does Prospero react to this intrusion?

_____

_____

15. Compare the movements of the intruder as he passes through the
rooms with those of Prince Prospero.

_____

_____

_____

16. What happens to Prince Prospero as he holds his dagger aloft within
a few feet of the intruder?

_____

17. How does Poe describe the emotional state of the masqueraders as
they rush upon the "mummer"?

_____

18. What happens when they try to grab his mask?

_____

19. What becomes of the revelers?

_____

Summarizing the Story

20. List the main events of the story in the order they happened.

_____

_____

_____

_____

_____

_____

Thinking About the Story

21. What is the theme of "The Masque of the Red Death"?

_____

Name   Class   Date

Julius Caesar: Act One
by William Shakespeare

Beginning Act One
Read all the information about the play given on pages 495 through 497 in your book. Then begin reading Act One. Read to the end of Scene 1, on page 501.

1. What two reasons, one humorous and one serious, does the Cobbler give Flavius for closing his shop?

2. Why does Marullus call the mob "senseless things!"? (lines 35-55)

3. What does Flavius tell the commoners to do?

4. How do the common folk react to the tribunes' words? (lines 56-60)

5. What do Marullus and Flavius undertake to do? (lines 63-75)

Continuing Act One
Read to the end of Scene 2, on page 510. Pay close attention to differences between Brutus and Cassius. Answer the questions below.

6. What does the Soothsayer tell Caesar to beware of, and how does Caesar respond?

7. What does Brutus perceive as a difference in character between Antony and himself? (lines 28-29)

8. What does Brutus reply when Cassius accuses him of behaving in a cold, strange manner?

9. Find one sentence spoken by Cassius that claims he sees Brutus' nobility better than Brutus himself can. (lines 66-78)

10. What types of weaknesses in Caesar does Cassius point out to Brutus in lines 100-131?

11. Do you think this weakness would hinder Caesar's ability as Roman emperor? Why or why not?

Name   Class   Date

12. In lines 162-175, how does Brutus react to Cassius' arguments against Caesar?

_____

_____

13. As Caesar and his retinue approach, how do they appear to Brutus?

_____

14. What type of man does Caesar tell Antony he wants around him? Why?

_____

_____

_____

15. Why does Caesar believe Cassius will never be "at heart's ease"? (lines 208-210)

_____

_____

16. How does Casca react to Antony's triple offer of kingship to Caesar? (lines 234-247)

_____

_____

_____

17. What chronic illness does Caesar suffer?

_____

18. What does Cassius plan to do to win Brutus' cooperation?

_____

_____

Continuing Act One

Read all of Scene 3, stopping on page 515. Answer the questions.

19. List a few of the strange things Casca has seen this night (lines 15-28) and tell what he thinks they signify (lines 28-32).

_____

_____

20. To whom does Cassius compare this strange and fearful night?

_____

21. What do the senators plan to do on the ides of March, according to Casca?

_____

22. Who does Cassius blame for Caesar's tyranny? (lines 103-115)

_____

23. Who do Cassius and Casca hope to win over to their plan before morning?

_____

Thinking About Act One

24. Match the character with the adjective that best describes him.

_____ Caesar   _____ Brutus   **a.** angry   **c.** arrogant

_____ Antony   _____ Cassius   **b.** cautious   **d.** obedient

Name   Class   Date

Julius Caesar: Act Two
by William Shakespeare

Beginning Act Two

   Although they are not major characters, Portia and Calpurnia do offer a female viewpoint on Rome's public affairs. Listen to them and remember that they would be "first ladies" in our culture. Read Scene 1.

   1. What is Brutus worried will happen if Caesar is crowned? (lines 10-34)

   _____

   _____

   2. What promise does Brutus make to Rome?

   _____

   _____

   3. To what does Brutus compare the mental anxiety he has been experiencing? (lines 60-69)

   _____

   4. Indicate below two words Brutus uses to describe conspiracy. (lines 77-85)

   _____

   5. What reason does Brutus give for not wanting to swear an oath to what they have resolved to do? (lines 114-119)

   _____

   _____

   6. What reason does Metellus give for wanting to include Cicero in their conspiracy? (lines 144-149)

   _____

   7. What reason does Brutus give for excluding Cicero? (lines 150-152)

   _____

   8. What does Brutus suggest they do about Antony? Why? (lines 162-183)

   _____

   _____

   9. Who among the men is not convinced by Brutus' argument?

   _____

   10. According to Decius, what is a sure-fire way to flatter Caesar?

   _____

   11. Portia is unhappy about Brutus' recent behavior (lines 237-256). What does she ask of him?

   _____

   12. What does Brutus tell her? (lines 305-309)

   _____

Continuing Act Two

   In Scene 2, notice the contrast between the relationships of Caesar and Calpurna and Brutus and Portia. Now read all of Scene 2.

Name   Class   Date

13. Just as Portia was concerned about Brutus' welfare, so too is Calpurnia concerned for Caesar. How does Calpurnia's concern differ from Portia's?

_____

_____

14. What does Caesar say that shows he views unrealistically his personal power in the face of danger? (lines 41-47)

_____

15. What reason does Caesar tell Decius to convey to the Senate for his not coming? (lines 71-79)

_____

16. Describe Calpurnia's dream as revealed by Caesar.

_____

_____

17. How is the dream interpreted by Decius? (lines 83-90)

_____

Continuing Act Two

    Read Scenes 3 and 4. Note how Shakespeare continues to build tension into the play so the audience will anticipate the climactic events in Act Three.

18. What does Artemidorus have for Caesar?

_____

19. Portia, in a very agitated state, sends Lucius to the Capitol to gather information. What does she want to know?

_____

Thinking About Act Two

20. To a greater or lesser degree, each of the characters below has knowledge of the conspiracy to kill Caesar that is afoot. Tell how each uses that knowledge in the play.

Portia: _____

_____

_____

Calpurina: _____

_____

_____

Artemidorus: _____

_____

_____

Name   Class   Date

Julius Caesar: Act Three
by William Shakespeare

Beginning Act Three

Read Scene 1. Pay close attention to what *is* said and what *is not* said.

1. Is Artemidorus successful in presenting his document to Caesar?

_____

2. What does Metellus ask of Caesar?

_____

3. What does Caesar's response to Metellus, Brutus, and the others tell
you about his self-image? (lines 55-70)

_____

4. Who is the first to stab Caesar? Who is the last?

_____

5. Why do you think Caesar stops defending himself when he sees the
dagger in Brutus' hand?

_____

_____

6. What does Brutus feel every Roman has gained by the assassination?
(lines 103-110)

_____

7. Cassius feels that the assassination of Caesar will go down in history.
How does he feel he and the other men will be remembered?

_____

8. What is Antony's attitude toward the conspirators? (lines 149-164)

_____

_____

9. Brutus attempts to explain their actions to Antony, offering brother-
ly love. What does Cassius offer Antony?

_____

10. Antony's second speech serves as a thinly veiled eulogy for Caesar.
To what does Antony compare the conspirators in this speech? (lines
195-211)

_____

11. What does Antony want to do with Caesar's body?

_____

12. How does Cassius react to this? What does Brutus resolve to do?
(lines 233-243)

_____

_____

13. After the conspirators leave, Antony prophesies over Caesar's body.
Summarize that prophecy in your own words. (lines 255-276)

_____

_____

_____

Name   Class   Date

Continuing Act Three

Read Scene 2. Antony's speech to the populace in this scene is one of the great masterpieces of persuasive rhetoric. Answer the questions below.

14. Note how Brutus builds his self-defense on two series of parallel statements. Fill in the conclusions to the second series.

There is tears for _____

joy for _____

honor for _____

death for _____

15. What does Brutus say he will do if the good of the country calls for it?

_____

16. What does Antony mean when he says, "I speak not to disprove what Brutus spoke, / But here I am to speak what I do know"? (lines 100-101)

_____

_____

_____

17. How is the crowd responding to Antony's speech?

_____

18. In refusing to read Caesar's will to the crowd, what frame of mind does Antony hope to transfer to them? (lines 127-136 and 140-145)

_____

_____

19. Which was "the most unkindest cut of all"?

_____

20. How does Antony suggest that the death of Caesar is the death of each individual Roman?

_____

21. In lines 207-225, Antony denies having the ability to "stir men's blood." Is this true?

_____

22. What do the citizens go off to do? (lines 250-256)

_____

Read all of Scene 3, then answer the question below.

23. Although there is some humor in the mistaken identity of Cinna here, this scene points up a serious development in Rome after the assassination. Antony had prophesied as much. What is this development?

_____

_____

Thinking About Act Three

24. Now that you have read Brutus' and Antony's speeches, who do you believe was in the right? Explain why on a separate sheet of paper.

Name	Class	Date

Julius Caesar: Act Four
by William Shakespeare

Beginning Act Four

Time has passed and Antony's prophecies have proven accurate. As you read, note how the main characters have changed. Read all of Scene 1, answering the questions below.

1. Do Antony's intentions for restoring peace and establishing a new Roman government seem honorable? Give evidence for your answer.

_____

_____

2. How does Antony intend to use Lepidus? (lines 18-27)

_____

_____

3. To what three things does Antony compare Lepidus?

_____

Continuing Act Four

Scenes 2 and 3 together parallel Scene 1. Since Caesar's death, Brutus has changed. So too, perhaps, will your impression of him. Brutus' transformation is the focus of *Julius Caesar*. Now read Scenes 2 and 3.

4. What has happened to the friendship of Brutus and Cassius?

_____

_____

5. What does Brutus say is a good indication of Cassius' change of heart? (lines 19-27)

_____

_____

6. Cassius greets Brutus with the accusation that Brutus has wronged him. Why does Brutus advise him to "Speak your griefs softly"?

_____

7. Why is Cassius angry with Brutus at the start of Scene 3? (lines 1-5)

_____

8. Why is Brutus angry with Cassius? (lines 9-12)

_____

9. Of what does Brutus remind Cassius in lines 18-28?

_____

_____

10. What additional transgression of Cassius' does Brutus reveal in lines 65-82?

_____

Name _____ Class _____ Date _____

11. Why does Cassius feel that Brutus is not treating him as a close friend?

_____

_____

12. Having denied Brutus gold, what does Cassius now offer Brutus? (lines 93-107)

_____

13. What purpose do you think the Poet serves in this scene?

_____

_____

14. Brutus tells Cassius of his sorrow. What is the cause, and how did it happen?

_____

_____

15. What does Messala indicate that Octavius, Antony, and Lepidus have done that shows the three have no intention of continuing a republican government?

_____

16. Give, in your own words, Brutus' reasons for proposing an attack against the triumvirate's forces.

_____

_____

_____

17. Find several details in lines 239-265 which show that Brutus is attempting to distance himself from the tensions of the anticipated attack.

_____

_____

18. Why do you think the Ghost of Caesar identifies himself as "Thy evil spirit, Brutus."

_____

_____

Thinking About Act Four

19. List one or more ways in which Brutus and Antony are alike.

_____

_____

_____

_____

_____

Name   Class   Date

Julius Caesar: Act Five
by William Shakespeare

Beginning Act Five
   Though this act brings you to the front lines of an historic battle, the
fighting and its results are not Shakespeare's main concern. Now comes
the culmination of the good and bad decisions these men have made;
strong personalities have brought themselves and the civilized world to
this crucial point. Read Scene 1, answering the questions below.

1. Who controls the army of the triumvirate, Octavius Caesar, Antony,
   or Lepidus? How do you know?

   _____

   _____

2. Do you think Antony's retelling of the assassination in lines 39-44 is
   accurate?

   _____

3. Cassius tells Messala that the day holds bad omens for their cause. If
   Cassius can only "believe it partly," why do you think he brings up
   these omens at all?

   _____

   _____

   _____

4. In lines 100-107, Brutus expresses his feelings concerning suicide.
   Write his opinion in your own words below.

   _____

   _____

5. Find one sentence that demonstrates Brutus' feeling that, one way or
   another, the events that they set in motion by killing Caesar will
   reach their conclusion this very day.

   _____

   _____

Continuing Act Five
   Read Scenes 2 and 3, then summarize below the events in their proper
order.

6. Write your summary on these lines.

   _____

   _____

   _____

   _____

   _____

   _____

   _____

   _____

Read Scenes 4 and 5, paying close attention to the "last words" of those who die. Pay equally close attention to the words of the survivors when they discover the deaths of their friends or enemies.

7. What qualities, admirable in a soldier, does Lucilius reveal in Scene 4?

_____

_____

8. What does Brutus whisper to Clitus and then to Dardanius?

_____

9. Rewrite the following lines in your own words: "Now is that noble vessel full of grief, / That it runs over even at his eyes." (lines 13-14)

_____

10. Why do you think Brutus believes that he will have "glory by this losing day / More than Octavius and Mark Antony" will in their victory? (lines 36-37)

_____

_____

_____

11. How does Brutus end his life?

_____

_____

12. Brutus' last words are addressed to Caesar. What do they mean?

_____

_____

13. Why does Antony believe Brutus was "the noblest Roman of them all"?

_____

_____

_____

Thinking About the Play

14. Do you think that assassination is ever justifiable as a means for political reform?

_____

_____

_____

_____

15. How do you think Shakespeare might have answered question **14**?

_____

_____

_____

Name   Class   Date

The Secret Room
by Corrie ten Boom

Beginning the Selection

War, danger, suspense, concealed doors, close calls, and secret organizations—Corrie ten Boom's true story has the necessary elements for a gripping tale. What sets it apart, however, is her ability as a writer to transfer these elements into effective language. Now read the selection to the paragraph that begins "When Fred opened the door" (page 605, column 1).

1. Describe the mood in Holland during the Nazi occupation.

_____

_____

2. Why is the public performance of "Wilhelmus" prohibited by the Nazis?

_____

3. What sound does Corrie identify with her enemies?

_____

4. What does Mrs. Kleermaker do which outwardly demonstrates that she is much afraid even after she is welcomed to the Beje?

_____

5. Find a sentence which gives the reason why the ten Boom family is willing to risk their safety for the fugitives who come to them.

_____

_____

6. What black market documents are most valuable to the underground movement of which Corrie has become a part?

_____

7. Why does Corrie's brother, Willem, refuse to help her?

_____

8. Why does Corrie hesitate to come straight to the point of her visit to Fred Koornstra?

_____

Continuing the Selection

Continue reading to the end of the selection. Find the secret room in the drawing of the Beje.

9. What does Fred do in order to continue supplying food ration coupons on a regular basis?

_____

10. Why does Corrie have such confidence that her needs will be supplied as long as the Beje is used as a hideout?

_____

_____

_____

Name   Class   Date

11. How does Corrie react upon entering the drawing room of the home
    in which the underground has gathered?

    _____

    _____

12. Find the paragraph that states the main business of the under-
    ground. Write down the first few words that identify this paragraph.

    _____

13. What code name identifies and protects members of the
    underground?

    _____

14. On the drawing, locate the "two old houses" that the architect finds
    so amazing. Why does he say that if all houses were made like
    these, he would be less worried?

    _____

    _____

    _____

15. Why is the false wall built out of brick instead of wood?

    _____

Thinking About the Selection

16. In what room in your home could a secret room be constructed? Ex-
    plain your choice of room and, on a separate piece of paper, draw a
    floor plan.

    _____

    _____

17. Corrie ten Boom was angered and worried by her nephew's defiance
    of the Nazis. Why does she later decide to harbor fugitives? Is she
    motivated by patriotism, by religion or by both? Do you think she
    may have other reasons? Explain your opinions.

    _____

    _____

    _____

    _____

    _____

    _____

    _____

    _____

    _____

Name   Class   Date

I Escape from the Boers
by Winston Churchill

Beginning the Selection

While Churchill is known worldwide as the greatest English-speaking statesman of the first half of the twentieth century, the general public remains less aware of his military exploits and of his considerable journalistic skills in recounting those adventures. Read up to the point at which Churchill, having escaped, "slept the sleep of the weary—but of the triumphant" (page 620, column 1).

1. What is the most critical detail of the escape planned by the prisoners?

_____

_____

2. What unknown makes the escape plan especially dangerous?

_____

_____

3. Why is Churchill in the "right mood" to go it alone after the other British prisoners are unable to follow him?

_____

4. List some of the immediate difficulties faced by Churchill which cause him to say that "hope had departed."

_____

_____

_____

_____

5. How does Churchill reach the conclusion that he has stolen aboard the train headed east as he had hoped?

_____

6. Why is Churchill physically unprepared for his long journey?

_____

7. What, more than anything else, makes Churchill miserable as he plods on toward Portuguese territory?

_____

_____

8. How does John Howard conceal his guest until arrangements have been completed for his journey?

_____

Continuing the Selection

Continue reading to the end of the selection. Answer the questions below.

9. Why does Howard have to go twenty miles to obtain a cooked chicken for Churchill's dinner?

_____

Name   Class   Date

10. Find a sentence in which Churchill comments that he would have felt more confident in escaping on his own, rather than hiding among bales of wool on a train.

_____

11. Churchill writes, "To be a fugitive . . . is a mental experience by itself." What does he mean by that?

_____

_____

_____

12. When the final journey begins on December 19, how many days have passed since Churchill escaped from the State Model Schools?

_____

13. How does Churchill occupy his mind during the first day of the train ride?

_____

_____

14. Why does Churchill try to keep from sleeping during his escape by train?

_____

15. Although the actual journey was expected to take sixteen hours, how long is it before Churchill emerges from his hiding place?

_____

16. What happens to Churchill when he arrives at the British Consulate?

_____

Thinking About the Selection

17. Could you have done the things that Churchill does in making his escape? Some but not all of them? Which ones? Why or why not?

_____

_____

_____

_____

_____

_____

_____

_____

_____

Name   Class   Date
_____

By Any Other Name
by Santha Rama Rau

Beginning the Selection

In one form or another you have probably heard the adage, "What's in a name? A rose by any other name would smell as sweet." As you read this selection, think about the significance of someone changing *your* name without your desire or consent. Now read all of the selection.

1. Find a sentence which shows that, during her tenure, the headmistress has not blended well with Indian culture.

_____

_____

2. Why have the two girls been sent to attend that particular Anglo-Indian day school?

_____

_____

3. How have the girls been educated before their attendance at the school?

_____

_____

4. At five years old Santha has a strange reaction to having her name changed. How does she describe that reaction?

_____

_____

5. Which features of the school building are Indian? Which are British?

_____

6. Why does Santha say that she doesn't know her own name when the teacher asks her what it is?

_____

_____

7. After the schoolchildren laugh at Santha for claiming not to know her own name, what does the little girl with the braids do which shows both her concern for Santha and her frustration with their position at school?

_____

8. Has Santha's home schooling been adequate? How do you know?

_____

9. Why does Santha have "no clear idea" of what winning means?

_____

_____

10. Why is Santha scolded for "not being a good sport"?

_____

11. What does Premila want to take to school in order to appear more British?

_____

Name _____ Class _____ Date _____

12. How would you describe Santha as a student?

_____

13. Why do you think "friendship with the English or Anglo-Indian children was out of the question"?

_____

_____

14. Why do you think Premila withholds from Santha the reason for their leaving school?

_____

_____

15. List several things Santha remembers about the long walk home from school.

_____

_____

_____

16. Why do you think Premila's mother is "silent a long time" before agreeing that her children should no longer attend the Anglo-Indian school?

_____

_____

17. To what does Santha attribute her lack of "psychological scars" from such a negative school experience?

_____

_____

Thinking About the Selection
18. What is Premila's attitude toward the school and the other children at first? Why does it change?

_____

_____

_____

_____

19. Why do you think the school headmistress changes Premila and Santha's names? Is it only because she can't pronounce them? What does the name change indicate about English attitudes toward the Indians?

_____

_____

_____

_____

_____

Name   Class   Date

First Lady Under Fire
by Margaret Truman

Beginning the Selection

   Though separated by more than a century, both author and subject
share an important kinship as former residents of the White House.
(Margaret Truman is the daughter of Bess Truman, First Lady during
the Truman administration.) Note the double meaning of the title as you
read the selection. Not only is Dolley Madison under literal fire from
British enemies, but the First Lady, as a public figure, is under the fire
of public opinion for the actions of her husband and herself. Read up to
the point at which two British deserters, when asked if their force is as
strong as the American army, reply, "We think it is" (page 637, column
2).

1. How does Dolley Madison use her name to resist the elitist attitudes
she finds in Philadelphia?

_____

2. How does Dolley Madison's Quaker upbringing help mold her adult
life?

_____

_____

3. What event, completely beyond her control, makes it possible for
Dolley Madison to become First Lady?

_____

4. Find two consecutive sentences which explain, in the author's eyes,
the distinctive trait in Dolley Madison's character.

_____

_____

5. Describe Dolley Madison's personality.

_____

_____

6. Why is the First Lady forced to cease decorating the "President's
Palace"?

_____

7. Who are the Federalists and why do they not support President
Madison at the start of the War of 1812?

_____

_____

8. How does the author describe the Washington of Dolley's day?

_____

9. What role does John Armstrong play in the British attack on
Washington?

_____

_____

Name   Class   Date

Continuing the Selection
   Now that the stage has been set, read the rest of the selection. Take careful note of the ways in which Dolley Madison reacts to news from the battlefront.

10. What "news leak" first causes panic to spread through the capital city?

_____

_____

11. Find one sentence in which the author reflects on one source for courage to survive a panic.

_____

_____

12. Which action taken by Dolley Madison does the author consider most significant in preserving the United States at such a critical time in its history?

_____

13. On August 24, what does the First Lady do to preserve morale after word of the American defeat reaches her?

_____

14. Why do you think the portrait of George Washington is so important to Dolley Madison?

_____

15. What was the effect on the American people of the British burning the White House?

_____

_____

16. Why do you think the author wants to attribute some of "the era of good feeling" to Dolley Madison? What does she mean by "the genius"?

_____

_____

_____

Thinking About the Selection
17. Find a sentence that indicates what it is that guides a courageous person's actions during conflict. Does the person always know the effect of his or her actions? How do Dolley Madison's actions under fire relate to her talents as a White House hostess?

_____

_____

_____

_____

_____

_____

Name   Class   Date

Four Letters

Reading the Letters

The authors of the following letters did not mean to write literary pieces when they sat down, pen in hand. We read these letters because they are literate communications from one individual to another, and because the individuals themselves are a part of our history.

Dolley Madison

1. To whom is Dolley Madison writing?

_____

2. Find a sentence which explains why the First Lady has to stir up a good deal of self-reliance during the military crisis she faces.

_____

_____

3. Why does Dolley Madison hesitate to leave Washington?

_____

4. What makes Dolley Madison's decisive effort to rescue George Washington's portrait significant?

_____

_____

Bartolomeo Vanzetti

5. Why does Vanzetti feel that he and Nicola Sacco are being persecuted?

_____

6. Give one of Vanzetti's reasons for writing to the young Dante.

_____

_____

7. Find two sentences in which Vanzetti uses exaggeration to emphasize the weakness of the evidence presented against Sacco and himself. Write down one of these exaggerations.

_____

_____

8. What does Vanzetti urge Dante to do?

_____

9. Vanzetti was obviously in an emotional frame of mind when he wrote this letter. From the tone and content of the letter, what impression do you form of his and Sacco's guilt or innocence? Why?

_____

_____

_____

_____

_____

_____

Name   Class   Date

Anne Morrow Lindbergh

10. What circumstances allow Anne to take the time to compose her letter?

_____

11. To what does Anne compare her sighting of the rainbow?

_____

12. List the words Anne uses to describe the cloud bank above which they are flying.

_____   _____

_____   _____

13. What is the origin and the destination of the flight?

_____

Harry S. Truman

14. Does President Truman feel as if he is making progress in his meetings? How do you know?

_____

_____

15. What fact does President Truman feel the need to repeat to his colleagues?

_____

16. What are the President's two goals for the meetings?

_____

_____

17. Find one sentence which shows that Truman feels that the meetings are difficult, but will be successful for America.

_____

_____

_____

Thinking About the Letters

18. Letters, because they are often written in haste and under duress (as these were) and because they are often intensely personal, tend to reveal the writer's personality and circumstances somewhat more than other forms of writing. This revealing of personality and circumstances in a person's writing can be referred to as his or her style. Of these four letters, the one in which the style is most evident is Truman's. Reread his letter, noting whatever seems unusual about his choice of words. What kind of person do you think Truman was? Describe his personality.

_____

_____

_____

_____

_____

Name   Class   Date

Three Days to See!
by Helen Keller

Beginning the Selection

Helen Keller was a remarkable woman. Never forget as you read that she was unable to see, unable to hear, and unable to speak before the age of sixteen. Her enthusiasm in this selection, therefore, is not a literary creation; rather, it is deeply and personally felt. Now read the entire selection.

1. Write down the topic sentence for this selection.

____ _____

_____

2. How does Helen experience trees, objects which sighted people tend to experience only through their vision?

_____

3. Why does Helen feel that sight must be such a marvelous sense to use?

_____

4. What emotions has Helen felt in her acquaintances through the use of touch?

_____

5. In what way does Helen feel that vision helps to understand other people?

_____

_____

6. Do you agree that most people "grasp only casually the outward features of a familiar face and let it go at that"? Why or why not?

_____

_____

7. Can you describe accurately, from memory, the face of one good friend? Try.

_____

_____

_____

8. What are Helen's subjects for her first day of vision?

_____

9. Why does Helen want to rise at dawn of the second day?

_____

10. What are Helen's subjects for her second day of vision?

_____

_____

Name _____ Class _____ Date _____

11. Why does Helen have a special affection for the Greek poet Homer?

_____

12. How does Helen come to the conclusion that dance must be a tremendously beautiful event to witness?

_____

_____

13. What are Helen's subjects for her third day of vision?

_____

_____

14. What very common scene does Helen speculate "must be a gorgeous spectacle"?

_____

15. Find a sentence that suggests the primary lasting value for using one's sight.

_____

_____

_____

16. Why does Helen feel that most people do not "really see"?

_____

_____

17. What advice does Helen Keller give to people who have no sense handicaps?

_____

_____

_____

Thinking About the Selection

18. Do you agree that sight is the "most delightful" of senses? Is lack of sight the worst handicap? Explain your answers.

_____

_____

_____

_____

19. Give a three-day "itinerary" if you could have a reprieve from some personal deficiency, physical or otherwise (e.g., poor athletic ability).

Day 1: _____

_____

Day 2: _____

_____

Day 3: _____

_____

Name   Class   Date

Grandmother Zabielska
by Zofia Starowieyska Morstin

Beginning the Selection

First, read the headnote for this selection. As you read all of the selection, make a mental note of the important lessons which the author has discovered about death and the family.

1. Why does their grandmother's death become "a kind of model death" for the children of the family?

2. What analogy does the author use to illustrate how the children judge an individual's lifespan against that of their grandmother?

3. Find a sentence in which the author comments that her grandmother's death is consistent with the manner in which she has lived.

4. Why is Grandmother Zabielska able to meet her death "reasonably"?

5. How does Grandmother Zabielska conduct herself during the progress of her illness?

6. In what way are "Emilia's people" unlike the Zabielskis?

7. What does Grandmother Zabielska mean when she says to Basia, "I know what I'm talking about. . . "?

8. What wish of Grandmother Zabielska's does Basia carry out even though it is against her natural inclination?

9. Why does Pani Liza find it hard to understand Grandmother Zabielska's peaceful acceptance of death?

10. Find a sentence in which Grandmother Zabielska explains why it is easy for her to leave the world of the living.

11. Find a sentence in which Grandmother Zabielska explains why it is easy for her to anticipate facing God's judgment.

Name   Class   Date

12. Do these attitudes of Grandmother Zabielska strike you as reasonable? Why or why not?

_____

_____

_____

13. What does the author choose as the most important aspect of Grandmother Zabielska's personality?

_____

14. How are the children brought indirectly into the experience of their
grandmother's dying?

_____

_____

15. How do the children participate directly in the actual event of their
grandmother's death?

_____

_____

16. What ancient Polish custom recognizes that even after the moment
of death the individual still retains an attachment to home and
family?

_____

_____

17. Describe the author's view of the proper environment for a human
being's death.

_____

18. Why do you think the author believes it is better to die "by God's,
not man's hand"?

_____

_____

Thinking About the Selection

19. Why do you think that the children of the Zabielski family look upon the death of their grandmother as a "good death"? How was the
children's attitude toward death "determined properly"?

_____

_____

_____

_____

_____

_____

Name   Class   Date

The Day We Flew the Kites
by Frances Fowler

Beginning the Selection

In this selection you will encounter two families in a particularly happy situation, one full of life and joy. The story is a celebration of family life over the time span of a generation. Read the entire selection, answering the questions below.

1. Why is Saturday such a busy day in the author's household?

_____

_____

2. What makes this particular Saturday busier than usual?

_____

_____

3. Find a sentence that explains why the women are ready to abandon their chores.

_____

_____

4. Do the author's mother and Mrs. Patrick feel comfortable at first about leaving their work to watch the boys fly their kites? How do you know?

5. Find a sentence in which exaggeration is used to emphasize the beauty of this particular spring day.

_____

6. Describe paper wishes.

_____

_____

7. To what does the author compare the children in the presence of their parents?

_____

8. Why do the children find it so remarkable that their parents are "really playing" with them?

_____

9. Why does the author think, though confusedly, that this may be like the Kingdom of Heaven?

_____

_____

10. Over the course of the years, what has the author forgotten about the day they flew the kites?

_____

11. Why do you think no one mentioned that day, afterward?

_____

_____

Name   Class   Date

12. Why does the author feel a little embarrassed?

_____

_____

13. Reread the paragraph beginning "A good many years had passed," on page 669. List several ways in which the author's situation differs from that of her mother.

_____

_____

14. What does her mother say that alters the author's approach to the day's duties?

_____

_____

15. What does the author mean by "the locked door flew open"?

_____

_____

16. What lesson has the author learned from this "little parable"?

_____

_____

17. a. How much time passes before the event involving the youngest Patrick boy takes place?

_____

    b. Why do you think the number of years is mentioned?

_____

18. How do the Patrick boy's experiences in a prisoner-of-war camp highlight, by contrast, his experiences on kite-flying day?

_____

_____

19. What event causes the reunion between the author and Mrs. Patrick?

_____

_____

Thinking About the Selection
20. Why do you think Mrs. Patrick is comforted by the memory that her husband had enjoyed "the day we flew the kites"? How do you think this makes the author feel?

_____

_____

_____

_____

_____

Name _____ Class _____ Date _____

My Store of Grievances
by John Welter

Beginning the Selection

First read the headnote. This selection defines by negation what a convenience store should be but, in the author's opinion, rarely is. By forming a composite of details most readers have encountered, Welter works toward a definition of the ideal convenience store. Now read the selection, but do not answer any of the following questions until you have finished.

1. Write down in order all of the signs the author would put up in and around his store.

   a. _____

   b. _____

   c. _____

   d. _____

   e. _____

   f. _____

   Now return to the beginning of the story. Answers to the remaining questions will occur sequentially in the text.

2. What do you think the author considers the most important qualities a convenience store should exhibit?

   _____

3. Find at least one sentence that implies how most convenience stores treat their customers.

   _____

4. Give the author's comic definition of a convenience store.

   _____

5. a. List the problems the author has with store clerks.

   1: _____

   2: _____

   3: _____

   4: _____

   b. List the opposite positive qualities the clerks should have.

   1: _____

   2: _____

   3: _____

   4: _____

Name _____   Class _____   Date _____

6. Why do you think the author bothers to bring up minor annoyances such as lids that do not fit the drinking cups or a lack of straws?

_____

_____

7. Does the author really believe that convenience store employees are as incompetent as the portraits he draws of them? How do you know?

_____

_____

8. In what sense does the convenience store management care about its customers?

_____

_____

9. How does the convenience store clerk treat the items the customer has purchased?

_____

10. a. What final "emotional touch" does the clerk add as the customer leaves the store?

_____

   b. What final "emotional touch" should the clerk add as the customer leaves the store?

_____

11. Explain how the title of this selection is a pun—a play on words. Which word has a double meaning?

_____

_____

12. Is "Get It and Get Out" a good name for the author's store? Why or why not?

_____

_____

Thinking About the Selection

13. Make a list of grievances you have against something with which you have regular contact.

   a. _____

   b. _____

   c. _____

   d. _____

   e. _____

Name   Class   Date

Biographies Bring New Companions
by Marchette Chute

Beginning the Selection
   Unlike the other selections in this unit, this is literature about literature. The author's purpose is not to entertain or exhort the reader but to
instruct the reader as to the merits of reading biographies. Now read the
entire essay, answering the questions below.

   1. What assumption does the author make at the very beginning of the
      essay?

   _____

   2. Is the author talking about "average" people? Explain.

   _____

   _____

   3. Throughout the essay the author states very clearly the positive qual-
      ities to be found in a good biography. Write the first of these.

      POSITIVE #1: _____

   _____

   4. What analogy does Chute use to express the manner in which a bi-
      ography reveals someone's life to the reader?

   _____

   _____

   5. Write down the next positive quality found in a good biography.

      POSITIVE #2: _____

   _____

   6. What major difficulty does the biographer of a dead individual face?

   _____

   _____

   7. Write down the next positive quality of a good biography.

      POSITIVE #3: _____

   _____

   8. How does the author define a great man?

   _____

   _____

   9. In what way is a biography a better representation of an individual
      than a portrait or bust?

   _____

   10. Write down the next positive quality of a good biography.

      POSITIVE #4: _____

   _____

Name _____ Class _____ Date _____

11. Write down the next positive quality found in a good biography.

    POSITIVE #5: _____

    _____

12. Write down the next positive quality of a good biography.

    POSITIVE #6: _____

    _____

13. Write down the next positive quality found in a good biography.

    POSITIVE #7: _____

    _____

14. Why do the biographies of Lincoln, Keats, Beethoven, and Milton help to give us a more balanced view of these great men?

    _____

    _____

15. Give one example of the kind of information the biography of William Shakespeare reveals about him which his own writings do not.

    _____

    _____

16. What is the ultimate biographical pleasure given to a reader?

    _____

    _____

Thinking About the Selection

17. Could a biography of an "average" person be as interesting as one of a famous person? Why or why not?

    _____

    _____

18. **a.** What might readers of your biography discover about you which they might never have known if they relied merely on "common knowledge" about you?

    _____

    b. Are all of these items things you would want to be widely known?

    _____

    c. Would you want the chance to read and edit your biography before it was published?

    _____

    d. If you edited a lot, would that make the biography less good?

    _____

    _____

Name   Class   Date

The Pearl: Chapter I
by John Steinbeck

Beginning Chapter I

In the two paragraphs preceding Chapter I, Steinbeck makes sure that his readers do not miss an important element of his novel—the fact that it is a parable. There are lessons to be learned that overshadow the importance of developing completely realistic characters or plot lines. As you read, stop long enough to think about what is happening and to whom. Read Chapter I to the end of the paragraph in which the scorpion first appears (page 695, column 1). Answer the questions below.

1. List several living things that Kino hears as he awakens.

_____

2. List one living thing that Kino sees as he awakens.

_____

3. What does Kino call the clear, soft song that plays in his head?

_____

4. Is Kino a contented man? Explain your answer.

_____

_____

5. Find a sentence that shows the horizons of Kino's life have been limited, and that change from the normal pattern is difficult for him. Write the first nine and last three words of it below.

_____

Continuing Chapter I

Read the rest of the chapter. Pay close attention to the information you are given about the doctor.

6. What new song comes to Kino? Why?

_____

_____

7. How does Juana act in the crisis? How do her actions differ from those of her husband?

_____

_____

_____

8. Name those in the "procession" to the doctor's office.

_____

_____

9. In the eyes of Kino, Juana, and their relatives and friends, what does the doctor represent?

_____

Thinking About Chapter I

10. What is your first impression of the town and its inhabitants? Answer the question on another sheet of paper.

Name   Class   Date

The Pearl: Chapter II
by John Steinbeck

Beginning Chapter II

Unlike the straightforward account of the simple daily existence of
Kino and his family in the first chapter, this one tells of mists, imagination, and local beliefs. Read the entire chapter, answering the questions
below.

1. In what sense is the air of the Gulf "uncertain"?

_____

_____

2. What makes Kino's canoe so valuable to him?

_____

3. Juana does not pray directly for Coyotito to be cured. What does
   she pray for?

_____

4. Steinbeck describes the process by which a pearl is made and comments briefly on the history of the pearl divers. He calls pearls "ac-
   cidents"; how does he describe the finding of a pearl?

_____

5. What song does Kino sing as he searches for oysters beneath the
   sea?

_____

6. What makes the melody of the song stronger than usual this
   morning?

_____

_____

7. What does Juana fear may happen if she wants something too much?

_____

8. Describe the pearl that Kino finds in the large oyster.

_____

9. What do Juana and Kino discover about Coyotito's condition?

_____

Thinking About Chapter II

10. Why do you think Kino acts as he does in the last paragraph of the
    chapter?

_____

_____

_____

_____

_____

_____

Name	Class	Date

The Pearl: Chapter III
by John Steinbeck

Beginning Chapter III

Now that Kino has found "the Pearl of the World," everyone in town is concerned that such good fortune will go to Kino's head. Whether their sentiments are sincere or merely the outgrowths of jealousy, neighbors and relatives all keep an eye on Kino and Juana. Do the same as you read, noticing how husband and wife cope with their new life. Begin Chapter III, stopping at the end of column 2, page 704.

1. How quickly had the news of the great pearl reached and spread through Kino's community?

2. How do the shopkeepers and the doctor react to the news of Juana and Kino's good fortune?

3. How does the pearl change the way the townspeople feel toward Kino and Juana?

4. List those dreams whose fulfillment Kino ties to the power of the pearl.

   a.

   b.

   c.

   d.

   e.

5. What will the neighbors, who now mark time from the day Kino found his pearl, say if Kino's plans come to nothing?

Continuing Chapter III

Continue reading until Kino becomes so uncertain about his present circumstances that "the music of evil throbbed in his head and nearly drove out Juana's song" (page 708, column 1).

6. How does Steinbeck characterize the priest who comes to see Kino and Juana?

Name _____ Class _____ Date _____

7. After the priest leaves, Kino is upset. He stands in the doorway, looking out into the night. List three natural sounds that reflect Kino's feelings.

a. _____ c. _____

b. _____

8. Kino has "made plans." According to the story, what do "the gods" think of men's plans?

_____

_____

9. What does the doctor give Coyotito?

_____

10. Where does Kino put the pearl?

_____

_____

11. Coyotito becomes very sick. Does Kino realize why? How do you know?

_____

_____

_____

Continue reading to the end of Chapter III.

12. The doctor comes to the house again, pretending he does not know that Kino has found the pearl. What does he offer to do with it?

_____

13. Now that the finding of the pearl is general knowledge, who does Kino fear?

_____

14. That night, as Kino and Juana lie on the sleeping mat, what do they hear?

_____

15. What does Kino do about it?

_____

16. What does Juana want to do with the pearl? Why?

_____

_____

_____

Thinking About Chapter III
17. More than once in this chapter Steinbeck calls Kino's pearl "The Pearl of the World." Since this novel is a parable, what do you think might be the significance of that title?

_____

_____

_____

_____

_____

Name   Class   Date

The Pearl: Chapter IV
by John Steinbeck

Beginning Chapter IV

In previous chapters Kino has been intimidated by the doctor's "knowledge." He is now about to be thwarted by the "knowledge" of the pearl buyers. Read through the description of the stout pearl buyer on page 716, column 1. Answer the following questions.

1. What is the town of La Paz humming about early the next morning?

2. What have the pearl buyers of the town agreed to do to Kino?

3. What do Kino's neighbors say they would do with the money if the pearl was theirs to sell?

4. What does Juan Tomás say to Kino that indicates none of the villagers have any idea what the pearl is worth?

5. How is this situation similar to that of Kino and the doctor in the previous chapter?

6. How had the priest explained the loss of the pearls when agents were sent to the capital to sell them?

7. What is your impression of the pearl buyer? Explain.

Continuing Chapter IV

Read to the end of the chapter, answering the questions below.

8. What does the dealer tell Kino about his pearl?

9. How do Kino's neighbors react after the dealer makes his offer and even suggests bringing in others to verify his appraisal?

10. Kino resolves to take the pearl to the capital. Steinbeck writes, "To determine to go and to say it was to be halfway there." Explain.

11. What does Juan Tomás give as the reason the villagers allow themselves to be cheated and bullied throughout life?

Thinking About Chapter IV
12. On a separate piece of paper, list the people you think might have attacked Kino. Discuss their motives.

Name   Class   Date

The Pearl: Chapter V
by John Steinbeck

Beginning Chapter V

The emotions in this chapter are intense and extreme; the actions are violent and decisive. As you read it, try to determine whether the outcome is inevitable. Read to page 722, column 2, through the paragraph that begins "He took his knife and left her." Answer the questions as you read.

1. What does Juana do in the moonlight?

   _____

2. Despite her pain at Kino's hand, Juana is not angry with her husband. She sees his obsession and rage as products of his maleness. What three female qualities does she feel may help her save her family?

   a. _____ b. _____ c. _____

3. What does Juana find in the path?

   _____

4. Kino declares that he killed only in response to a personal attack. Why does Juana insist that they leave, rather than stay and explain his action?

   _____

   _____

5. What "last thing" has happened to tighten Kino "beyond breaking"?

   _____

   _____

Continuing Chapter V

Read the rest of the chapter, answering the questions below as you read.

6. What happens to Kino and Juana's brush house?

   _____

7. Where do Juana and Kino go to hide in preparation for their escape?

   _____

8. Much trouble has spread through the village because of Kino. To what does Kino compare himself?

   _____

9. Kino states that the pearl now "is my misfortune and my life and I will keep it." Find a sentence showing how closely he now identifies all that he is with the pearl.

   _____

   _____

Thinking About Chapter V

10. Why do you think Kino turns on Juana with such violence when, at the beginning of the chapter, she tries to throw the pearl into the water? Answer the question on a separate sheet of paper.

Name	Class	Date

The Pearl: Chapter VI
by John Steinbeck

Beginning Chapter VI

This chapter begins much as the first chapter, with a description of the physical environment. Now, however, the setting reflects the fierceness of an alien and unfamiliar world. Read up to the point where Kino sees the dark man whose "rifle gleamed in the sun" (page 728, column 1).

1. As Kino and Juana make their escape, Kino feels something stirring in himself. What is it?

_____

_____

2. What are the songs Kino now hears?

_____

3. Why does Kino believe that the pearl really is valuable in spite of what the pearl buyers told him?

_____

4. Kino repeats the prophecies he made over the pearl in Chapter III. What real events does he see as he now gazes into the pearl?

Instead of: Kino sees:

   a. _____   _____

   b. _____   _____

   c. _____   _____

5. How has the music of the pearl changed?

_____

6. In the distance Kino sees three men. What are they looking for?

_____

Continuing Chapter VI

This section of Chapter VI is filled with suspense. Read to the point at which Juana tells Kino to "Go with God" (page 732, column 1).

7. What simile does Steinbeck use to describe the trackers as they approach?

_____

8. Afraid the trackers will find and kill them, Kino and Juana try to escape. Where do they head?

_____

9. Find the paragraph on page 729 which begins "And Kino fled." What does Kino "see" as the outcome of their escape? Is his vision very detailed?

_____

10. What does Juana say three times to Kino that gives him strength?

_____

11. What do the couple find in the mountain cleft?

_____

Name   Class   Date

12. In what sense are "the little pools of water" places both of life and of death?

13. Kino estimates the three men will reach him and his family by what time?

14. As two men sleep and the third watches, what does Kino resolve to do?

Before finishing this story, think about how you expect it to end. Write your ending in the space below, then finish *The Pearl*.

15. Write your ending below.

16. To what is Kino compared as he sneaks up on the trackers?

17. A cry is heard. What does one man think it may be? What does the rifleman do?

18. When Kino attacks, what has he ultimately become because of the pearl?

19. After Coyotito's death, Kino and Juana return home. Find a sentence that shows once again how the physical environment reflects the realities in their lives. Write it below.

20. What do you think is the meaning of Steinbeck's statement that Kino and Juana "had gone through pain and had come out on the other side"?

21. When Kino looks at the pearl for the last time, what has it become?

22. What is the predominant color used in the final two paragraphs? Why do you think Steinbeck might have used it?

Thinking About the Story

23. Juana tells Kino that Coyotito will not cry when the trackers are near because "He knows." Some form of that phrase occurs often in *The Pearl*. On a separate sheet of paper, discuss the kind of knowing this is.

Name   Class   Date

Master and Man: Chapters I, II, and III
by Leo Tolstoy

Beginning the Story: Chapter I

Before beginning the story, read the Comment on page 739 to gain some insight into the life of the Russian peasant in the nineteenth century. The action in this story unfolds slowly, so be patient. Now read only the first chapter, answering the questions below.

1. As the story begins, what is the month and the decade?

2. In what country does the story take place?

3. If the ruble at the time of the story was worth about fifty cents, what was the value in dollars of the timber Vassili hoped to purchase?

4. Describe Nikita in your own words.

5. Although Nikita knew he was often cheated by Vassili, why did the servant continue to stay with his master?

6. How does Nikita speak to the cob, Brownie?

7. Tolstoy describes Vassili's wife and son in identical terms. Find the description and write it below.

8. What does Vassilia Andreitcha implore her husband to do? Why?

9. Why doesn't Nikita change his inadequate boots?

Continuing the Story: Chapter II

As you read Chapter II, notice how Nikita reacts when Vassili does not accept his suggestions for their route. Read the entire chapter, answering the questions below.

10. What are the weather conditions as the two men begin their journey?

Name   Class   Date

11. How do you know that Vassili considers his traveling companionship
with Nikita as a compliment to the servant?

_____

_____

12. What is Nikita's attitude toward his wife?

_____

_____

13. What is the passion that completely absorbs Vassili?

_____

14. Vassili suggests a route that passes by Karamishevo. Nikita agrees
this route would be the easier. Why do you think Vassili chooses another route instead?

_____

_____

15. The travelers lose the road. Where do they find themselves, according to Nikita?

_____

16. Who eventually finds the road again?

_____

Continuing the Story: Chapter III

For a moment Vassili's personal discomfort overcomes his pride, and
he allows Nikita and the cob to have their way. The result is a pleasant
stop in a cheery village. Read all of Chapter III, answering the questions
below.

17. What does Vassili's friend Isai advise him to do?

_____

18. What is the whirling black thing they meet up with on the road?

_____

19. How does each man react to the "contest" they engage in?

Nikita: _____

Vassili: _____

20. The sledge leaves the road again, and Brownie again manages to find
it. Where do they find themselves half an hour later?

_____

21. What advice does the old man give Vassili?

_____

22. From what book does Petrushka quote? Why does he quote this particular book?

_____

Thinking About the Chapters
23. Now that Vassili and Nikita have come to a place of warmth, safety,
and companionship for the evening, what do you think will happen
next? Write your answer on another sheet of paper.

146

Name   Class   Date

Master and Man: Chapters IV, V, and VI
by Leo Tolstoy

Continuing the Story: Chapter IV
Read the entire chapter, answering the questions below as you read.

1. What makes the household in which Vassili and Nikita find themselves so "rare"?

2. What is Nikita's response when he is offered a glass of vodka?

3. On page 755, both the old man of the house and Vassili use the word *business*, but in two different ways. Explain the difference.

4. What is the subject of the discord in the old man's family?

5. Is Vassili confident that they will be able to complete their journey?

6. Why does Nikita keep to himself his objections to setting out again?

Continuing the Story: Chapter V
Read all of Chapter V, making a special effort to picture the situation in which the two men find themselves. Answer the questions below.

7. The men reach the turning. In which direction does Petrushka ride?

8. Find a sentence that shows how much alike Nikita and Brownie are in their manner of serving their master.

9. What happens to Nikita as he leaps from the sledge to see why Brownie has stopped?

10. Find a sentence that shows how much alike Vassili and Brownie are in their reliance upon Nikita.

11. After Nikita returns and finds Vassili, what does Vassili at long last say they must do?

12. As the men struggle through the snow, how has their relationship changed significantly?

Name   Class   Date

13. What is Nikita's attitude toward the prospect of freezing to death?

_____

Continuing the Story: Chapter VI
  Vassili and Nikita now realize they must spend the night in the blizzard. Does either of the two think more about himself than about his companion? Read the entire chapter, answering the questions below.

14. What does Vassili do while Nikita makes the distress signal?

_____

_____

15. Whose welfare is Nikita's first concern as they prepare to "dig in" for the night?

_____

16. What does Vassili think about as he beds down in the sledge?

_____

17. When Vassili's wife comes to mind, in what light does he see her?

_____

18. Circle the one piece of property named below that Vassili *doesn't* own.

  a mill   two rented holdings   a villa

  two taverns   a granary   a lumberyard

19. Find one sentence indicating that Vassili is beginning to believe their predicament is Nikita's fault.

_____

20. In spite of Nikita's cleverness and adaptability, why do you think Vassili still calls the *muzhiks* "a stupid lot—a mere welter of ignorance"?

_____

21. When Vassili is finally able to read his watch, what time is it?

_____

22. Crazed with fear, Vassili thinks of mounting the horse and riding off. How does he rationalize leaving Nikita alone?

_____

_____

Thinking About the Chapters
23. Vassili's sense of well-being throughout the story comes from his thoughts about business. Yet as he sits in the frozen night trying to think of "his business affairs and accounts, his reputation, dignity, and wealth, the more did terror begin to master him." Why do you think he cannot drive away his fear?

_____

_____

_____

_____

Name   Class   Date

Master and Man: Chapters VII, VIII, IX, and X
by Leo Tolstoy

Continuing the Story: Chapter VII
   This chapter focuses on Nikita—his inner strengths and weaknesses. Read the entire chapter, answering the questions below.

1. In the first paragraph, Nikita takes stock of his situation. Why is he not afraid to die?

_____

_____

_____

2. At the end of the previous chapter, Vassili assumed that Nikita was shouting after him to come back with Brownie and not to leave him alone. What was Nikita really shouting about?

_____

_____

3. Nikita does not succumb to fear as did Vassili. What knowledge brings him comfort?

_____

_____

Continuing the Story: Chapter VIII
   Simply put, Vassili's panic has got him going round in circles, both physically and mentally. Read the entire chapter, answering the questions below.

4. What is the moving black object that appears before Vassili?

_____

5. What does Vassili realize when he sees tracks in the snow?

_____

6. Find a sentence which shows that, unlike Nikita, Vassili believes himself to be utterly alone.

_____

_____

7. Nikita was concerned for his soul; what is Vassili concerned about?

_____

8. What relationship does Vassili see between religion and himself in the paragraph that begins "O Queen of Heaven!" (page 773)?

_____

_____

_____

9. Where has Vassili followed Brownie to?

_____

Name   Class   Date

Continuing the Story: Chapter IX

This chapter contains the climax of Tolstoy's story. Read the entire chapter, answering the questions below.

10. What is the first thing Vassili does which is for someone or something other than himself?

_____

11. What does Nikita say that acts as a key to the change that takes place in Vassili? Why do you think Nikita's words are so important?

_____

_____

12. What does Vassili do next, with the same "air of decision" as when he "struck hands over a good bargain"?

_____

13. While he exerts his remaining mental and physical energy to save Nikita, what does Vassili experience as if for the first time?

_____

14. Vassili says, "Nikita, my old friend, I thought we were done for. You would have been frozen, and I—" How do you think Vassili would have finished his sentence had he been able to?

_____

15. What does Vassili keep asking his wife?

_____

16. Who is the Man Vassili waits for in his dream? What does he say to this Man?

_____

_____

Continuing the Story: Chapter X

As the novel ends, it is evident that events have turned out well for Nikita. They have turned out well for Vassili Brekhunoff also! Read to the end of the story. Answer the remaining questions.

17. Nikita dreams of a burden on his back. What is this burden in reality, and why does it get heavier?

_____

18. What has become of Vassili?

_____

19. Does Nikita change after the ordeal he has undergone? Explain.

_____

20. How many more years does Nikita live?

_____

21. Describe the circumstances of Nikita's death.

_____

_____

Thinking About the Story

22. On a separate piece of paper, discuss why you think Tolstoy titled his novel *Master and Man*.

Answer Key

Unit 1 Traditions in the Short Story

Page 1 The Conjurer's Revenge
1. magician   2. "Oh, how wonderful! How does he do it?"   3. He says that the conjurer had the object up his sleeve.   4. They agree with the Quick Man's explanation.   5. His reputation has sunk to zero.   6. They are: a gold watch, which he pounds to pieces; a handkerchief, which he punches holes into; a silk hat, which he dances on and crushes; and a celluloid collar, which he burns with a candle.   7. The Quick Man believes that the conjurer will simply use these things in his performance, and that he will return them unharmed.   8. He has in fact destroyed all the possessions the Quick Man has given him.   9. Answers will vary, but most students will agree that the Quick Man deserved what he got for the way he ruined the conjurer's show.

Page 3 The Monkey's Paw
1. The blinds are drawn and a fire burns brightly; a father and son play chess while a white-haired lady knits.   2. White complains about living in a slushy, out-of-the-way place in which the "pathway's a bog, and the road's a torrent." His wife thinks he's angry about losing the chess match.   3. They treat him well, offering drinks and a seat by the fire, and listening eagerly to his stories.   4. Morris at one time worked in the same warehouse as White.   5. to show that fate ruled people's lives, and that interfering with fate would only lead to sorrow   6. throw the paw away or destroy it   7. He wishes for two hundred pounds; his son suggests the wish.   8. The monkey's paw has moved in his hands.   9. Mrs. White   10. because it is two hundred pounds, the exact amount their son had told them to wish for   11. "Sometimes they hardly exchanged a word, for now they had nothing to talk about, and their days were long to weariness."   12. She decides they must wish their son alive again.   13. He is "aghast," but he does as she asks.   14. The paw once again moves in Mr. White's hand when he makes the wish.
15. the cemetery   16. that the thing at the door be sent back to where it came from   17. because he is deathly afraid his wife will open the door to behold their maimed, decomposing son   18. Answers will vary, but it would seem that it has. The monkey's paw allowed only three wishes, and all have been made. However, there is no telling what may happen when the paw falls into new hands.

Page 5 The Adventure of the Blue Carbuncle
1. Commissionaire Peterson witnessed a gang attempting to rob a man carrying a goose. As the men struggled, the commissionaire's presence scared the owner of the goose. The man dropped the goose and lost his hat, both of which the commissionaire recovered and brought to Holmes.
2. Three of the following may be listed.

FEATURE:	SIGNIFICANCE:
large size	an intelligent man
expensive hat, but worn	man was wealthy but has fallen on hard times
house dust	man goes out little, has unloving wife
moisture marks	man is out of shape
ink on felt	man has self-respect

3. by the card on the bird's leg that says, "For Mrs. Henry Baker"   4. a blue stone; found in the crop of the goose   5. Its value can only be guessed; it is so unique as to be priceless.   6. A plumber, John Horner, was accused by the head attendant of the Cosmopolitan Hotel, James Ryder, of stealing the blue carbuncle from the Countess of Morcar's jewel case. The plumber had been brought to the Countess's room in order to solder a loose bar in the grate.   7. that Baker is a poor man to whom the loss of hat and goose is a heavy one; he will surely attempt to recover them
8. The stone is twenty years old; it was found in southern China by the Amoy River.   9. *Baker:* He bought the goose at the Alpha Inn. *landlord:* He bought his geese from Breckinridge. *Breckinridge:* A number of people had already inquired about his source for the geese, which he bought from Mrs. Oakshott.   10. the cut of his whiskers and *The Sporting Times* sticking out of his pocket   11. Catherine Cusack   12. How did the carbuncle come to be swallowed by the goose?
13. "This fellow will not go wrong again; he is too terribly frightened. Send him to jail now, and you make him a jail-bird for life."   14. Accounts will vary, but should be written from the very limited perspective of an innocent man unaware of the intrigue around him.

Page 7 The Parachutist
1. The hawk was unable to hunt during the hurricane, and food is now scarce.   2. It is very good at spotting small signs of life; it carefully studies every detail of the environment below.   3. The kitten is leaping and tumbling playfully, without a care in the world. The hawk is intent, driven to find food.
4. No, it is startled but unaware of the danger it is in.   5. that the hawk is its only contact with solidity and safety   6. It is a parachutist in the sense that it hangs on for dear life as the hawk descends three hundred feet. It becomes a pilot when it secures a better foothold and rides the hawk in a slow glide to earth.   7. possibly that the kitten has no understanding of what has just taken place, and is going about its regular business; possibly that it is so overcome by its experience that it needs the comfort of a friendly voice   8. Answers will vary, but should probably include the observation that the kitten was a good choice because it is an animal most readers would feel sympathy toward—young, small, familiar, innocent—making its plight the more dramatic and wrenching for the reader.
9. Again, answers will vary. Some students will assert that hate is strictly a human emotion—that animals react only according to instinct. Others may argue that animals can experience intense emotions—ranging from what appears to be extreme happiness to something similar to rage, hate, or even grief.

Page 9 The Secret Life of Walter Mitty
1. It causes him to drive his car too fast.   2. Mrs. Mitty   3. By not revealing Mitty's occupation, Thurber never allows the reader to envision him as

competent at anything; an occupation in which he is given rigidly defined tasks to perform that don't require great concentration. **4.** because his wife has mentioned that she'd like Dr. Renshaw to look him over **5.** He is a millionaire banker and a close personal friend of Roosevelt. **6.** because a coreopsis is a kind of flower **7.** Yes. Mitty is, in fact, incompetent in some ways. Mrs. Mitty tries to protect him from himself, as a mother might a young child. **8.** "Perhaps this will refresh your memory." **9.** his calling the District Attorney a "miserable cur " **10.** "pocketa-pocketa-pocketa" **11.** When Mitty states that, as his wife had requested, he has bought overshoes, she answers, "Couldn't you have put them on in the store?" **12.** They all place him in a position of great personal responsibility, involving risk. Other people are very dependent on his knowledge and expertise to save the day. **13.** his own execution; answers will vary: no, this is the only fantasy in which he doesn't triumph; yes, he seems to have little control over his daydreams, and will no doubt slip into them again **14.** Answers will vary, but should include mention of the fact that most of us can identify with a daydreamer, particularly one presented in such a humorous way.

Page 11   A Visit to Grandmother

1. He is the warmest of men; kind; makes people relax, even laugh; cares about people. **2.** "I wanted to go to school. They didn't have a Negro high school at home." **3.** a very warm and loving reception; she hugs him and asks how he is **4.** "When I want help, I'll let you know. Only time I'll need help getting anywhere is when I dies and they lift me into the ground." **5.** "His father only spoke when he was spoken to, and then only one word at a time, as if. . . he had become a small boy again, . . . while his mother spoke with her guests." **6.** GL **7.** He is undisciplined and somewhat thoughtless; he is being protected because he is "family." **8.** No, both he and the horse trader were cheating each other. **9.** He tells her he can't because he doesn't know where to find the trader. **10.** She thinks it was drugged to appear docile, and the drug is now wearing off. **11.** Mama does what she feels will make GL happy. **12.** She says ". . . I was a mother and my baby asked me to do something, is all." **13.** Charles says that if he had been in GL's place, he would have been beaten for it. **14.** He says that it cannot be true, and begs her to admit it. He refuses to believe that he misread his mother's intentions. **15.** Either choice is acceptable. GL has been spoiled all his life, but he is not a mean person; he has been protected from life in a way that Charles never was. **16.** Dr. Dunford felt that his mother was distant, severe, unfair, intimidating, and unloving. Knowing what a devastating effect his mother had on him, he has tried to cultivate the opposite virtues. **17.** Charles thinks it is too late for his mother to start loving him "properly." No. Mama did love him, and it is never too late to talk out a misunderstanding when the love actually exists.

Page 13   The Other Wife

1. Alice feels more at ease. Marc tightens his grip on her arm and shushes Alice. **2.** his first wife **3.** incompatibility **4.** She has dark, smooth hair, blue eyes, is relaxed and smoking. She seems sophisticated, controlled, aloof, cool, a loner. **5.** She is pretty, has put on weight, has blue eyes, golden hair, is immodest, happy, and grateful to her husband. She seems to lack sophistication. **6.** He did not succeed in making his first wife happy. **7.** Alice begins to wonder if Marc is less than "perfect" after all. Perhaps she should be more cautious in her submissiveness toward him. **8.** Answers will vary, but some students may foresee trouble now that Alice's illusion of Marc has been disturbed.

Page 15   The Boar Hunt

1. None is English; they are all from South America; they work together on a sugar plantation; they enjoy debate; they hunt for sport. **2.** The area east of the Andes is characterized by fertile plateaus and untouched jungles. **3.** money, rifles, munitions, boots, hammocks **4.** "We had been informed that boars travel in herds of several thousands . . . organized just like an army." **5.** no roads; unexplored underbrush; imposing jungles; "careful not to lose ourselves in the thicket"; heat was great **6.** They are afraid of the unknown, and look to their weapons and one another for support and protection. **7.** hearing: strange noises; distant, sudden sound of rustling branches; the sound again **8.** They are elated. They shoot at the boars. **9.** A herd of boars numbers in the thousands. A herd's marching in closed ranks is a sign of their hunger and viciousness. **10.** They wonder what would happen to a man who fell within their reach. **11.** The hunters begin to relax as they eat and smoke in their hammocks. Meanwhile, the boars are as intense as ever. **12.** The hunters anxiety increases with the darkness. They are aware of the slaughtered boars and of the continuing activity of the rest of the herd. **13.** They have been digging around the trunk of the tree, gnawing the roots. **14.** The boars' attack is instinctual, persistent, and methodical; the hunters' attack was preconceived, swift, and random. **15.** They believe the boars are seeking revenge for man's ruthless killing of animals. **16.** It is instinctual, a reviving of "habits which the species had forgotten." **17.** He will no longer hunt animals for pleasure. He will reluctantly help exterminate harmful beasts. **18.** Answers will vary.

Page 17   Life Is Sweet at Kumansenu

1. It is a small village, cleared from the edge of a rain forest, and near the sea. The houses are square and made of mud, with roofs like helmets. **2.** They died. **3.** a spirit-child. **4.** He advises that she mangle it and break its bones in order to stop its reappearance. No, she marks its buttock instead. **5.** He is grayish brown and handsome. He wears a short-sleeved, opened-necked white shirt, gray gabardine trousers, a gold watch, and brown suede shoes. He has a large handkerchief tied round his neck. **6.** She is to tell absolutely no one of his visit. **7.** He seems to be referring to something unfortunate, perhaps tragic, that has befallen him. (We will surely learn more as the story progresses.) **8.** They ascend into a hilly region on a clear day. It is an idyllic setting, a pastoral scene in which father and daughter are literally above the everyday world of the village. **9.** The student should sense by this time that Meji is dead; for him, the world ended at noon on Friday. **10.** because Meji is now passing into his father's world; he is more spirit than he is "flesh" **11.** "... he felt nearer his father at that moment than he had ever done before in his life." **12.** Meji has not been eating, and there is a smell of decay in his room. **13.** It is raining heavily and lightning flashes periodically. **14.** Asi observes that he was wearing a scarf around his neck, and she knows the special way to open the locket. **15.** Meji was a mocking spirit who should have been destroyed thirty-one years ago. **16.** Meji had led a good life these thirty-one years, becoming much-respected among the villagers. He had produced a daughter (can spirits reproduce?), and his death was purely accidental. Finally, he felt the very urgent need to thank his mother "for giving me a chance." If he has become a spirit, he is certainly not a mocking one. **17.** Answers will vary. Many students will say no, because much of the effect of the story depends on the uncertainty as to whether Meji was a spirit-child, the living proof of the truth of local legends. Modern America would not lend itself to a set of such legends from which the story could develop. Others will argue that similar myths and legends abound in this country, what some call urban folk tales, and that this story could easily be rewritten to take place in Manhattan.

Page 19   Home
1. this porch; snake plant in the jardiniere in the southwest corner; obstinate slip from Aunt Eppie's magnificent Michigan fern at the left side of the friendly door; their rocking chairs; late afternoon light on the lawn; emphatic iron of the fence; poplar tree **2.** because they may be forced to move if they do not get another extension on the payment of a homeowner's loan **3.** She is trying to keep a rein on her emotions. She wishes to preserve the peace and beauty of what might be the last day of "owning" this place she loves. **4.** She mentions beautiful times in spring and autumn, when all have enjoyed building a "little fire in the fireplace," when the others are trying to think positively about leaving. **5.** the senses of sight and hearing: she is emphasizing the differences between their present neighborhood and South Park **6.** "Her [mama's] eyes were lamps turned on." **7.** Each student's answer will be drawn from personal experience.

Page 21   Forgiveness in Families
1. She says exactly what she thinks, in whatever order it occurs to her to say it. She is informal and not lacking in opinions. **2.** He was born on her first day of school; he threw up at her wedding; he stayed home from school for weeks on end with asthma; he sold *Gateways to Bookland* for ten dol-

lars; he was involved in a cheating ring and was expelled from school; he can't keep a job. **3.** Cam has taken the easy way out in most situations, has lacked responsibility, and has done whatever he pleased for most of his life. **4.** She is forgiving of them, and seems to find them amusing. She feels that he has had a rough time in life because of his asthma and lack of a father. **5.** "Referring to the girl who came and told us she had been engaged to him. . . . Mother said it was a lie told out of kindness. I said . . . she would have been supporting him for the rest of his life." **6.** Answers may vary, but most will agree that he does seem immature and irresponsible for someone his age. **7.** Val partially attributes her mother's illness to the vegetarian diet Cam convinced her to start. **8.** Yes. He cannot handle situations that call for facing unpleasantness or pain. **9.** "And I thought, all these things don't seem much like life, when you're doing them, they're just what you do . . . in life." **10.** Haro feels that despite Cam's peculiarities he is still a member of the family and should be kept informed. **11.** Cam had been with the members of his religious cult "working" for his mother's return to health. **12.** " 'Now where's her room?' says Cam in a practical tone of voice." **13.** Much of her life Val has been waiting for Cam to suffer for the way he has lived, for his carelessness and neglect, yet he has always come away unhurt and unpunished. Some part of her is sorry he didn't actually cause their mother's death and won't suffer the consequences. **14.** Cam thinks about adopting a more "common" lifestyle, but there is no suggestion in the story that this change is any more than another fad. **15.** Val learns that no one in a family is perfect; that she herself is not without mean, petty impulses; and that the measure of forgiveness resides in allowing a person to be who he or she is.

Page 23   Lamb to the Slaughter
1. She seems to be a typical urban housewife. She is calm and content. She is six months pregnant. **2.** because when he comes home it is "a blissful time of day"; she loves to "luxuriate in the presence of this man . . ." **3.** She loves the way he sits in a chair, the way he comes in a door, moves across a room, the intent far look in his eyes, the shape of his mouth, and his silence. No, they seem superficial—almost as though she can find nothing else to love about him or doesn't care to know him any more deeply. **4.** He is tired, troubled, and a policeman. **5.** They go out to dinner. **6.** Mary is attempting to put a difficult situation back on a normal track; she falls back on what she knows best and on what has probably appeased her husband in the past. **7.** probably that he wants a divorce, certainly that he is leaving her **8.** She hits him on the back of his head with a frozen leg of lamb. **9.** She is very matter-of-fact about it; she begins to plan the cover-up. **10.** to build an alibi and to try to regain some sense of the normalcy she had enjoyed before the murder **11.** She feels that in doing so there will be no need for acting when she sees his body and confronts the police.

12. No, she is used to fooling herself about things—the happiness of her marriage, for example. 13. two policemen (Noonan and O'Malley), a doctor, two detectives, a police photographer, and a man who "knew about fingerprints" 14. finding the murder weapon ("Get the weapon, and you've got the man.") 15. She knows they won't find "the heavy blunt instrument" they are looking for; she knows she has an excellent alibi in the grocer's statements; and she is friends with the policemen doing the investigating. 16. She gives them whiskey and invites them to dinner. 17. because the men are discussing the murder weapon even as they consume it—it is literally under their noses 18. Answers will vary. 19. Answers will vary.

Page 25 Through the Tunnel
1. Jerry has led a very safe, protected life, the life of the familiar beach. Out beyond him is the rest of life, the wild and dangerous bay. It is inviting yet frightening. 2. She is very eager to accommodate him; she has been protective but feels he should be given some freedom. 3. because he has chosen a path down which, literally and figuratively, his mother will never travel; he has left her behind 4. They are naked; he is not. He is English; they are not. They are noisy; he is not. They are friends; he is alone. They are older than he. 5. They are in the water, swimming through the tunnel in the rock. 6. He cries because he believes the boys have left to get away from him and because he has not been able to join their ranks as a swimmer of underwater caves. 7. Possible answers: Jerry is growing up and his mother's influence is diminishing. Jerry begins to see the "smallness" of the life he has lived with his mother. 8. The salt water hurts his eyes and prevents clear vision. It is important that he see clearly what he is getting himself into. 9. He must be able to stay under water for a long time. He must discover the way through the rock. 10. He holds on to a large stone and stays under water as long as he can. 11. His nose bleeds. 12. It has come to represent a childish place, a place of his youthful past. He now has more pressing, manly business to attend to in the water off the rocky bay. 13. He recognizes that if he doesn't go he will regret it all his life, and that his failure to act now will make it all the harder to act in the future. 14. She has Jerry marking time under water and repeating one hundred and fifteen over and over. 15. because Jerry has done what he set out to do there; he does not need to return to prove himself, as he had on the days before 16. The rock may represent any barrier that stands between ourselves and our dreams. It may represent the obstruction between the known and the unknown or the hurdle to be crossed from childhood to adulthood. There are any number of similar possibilities. 17. Answers will vary according to personal experience.

Page 27 The Story of the Widow's Son
1. She tells the reader that the story has two endings. 2. She walks the cow along the wayside grass; she walks to town and back to sell cabbages; she gets up at dawn to gather mushrooms; she sells eggs. 3. He is studious, tall, with strength of character. 4. The neighbor adds a hint of apprehension to the story by pointing out ways in which Packy might have been harmed on any given day while coming home from school. 5. While riding down a hill on his bike, he tries to avoid hitting a hen, is thrown off the bike, and is killed. 6. "Why did he put the price of an old clucking hen above the price of his own life?" 7. that he is the spoiled only child of a doting widow-mother 8. "Packy cowered down over the carcass of the fowl and hunched up his shoulders as if to shield himself from a blow." 9. She doesn't want the neighbors to think she treats her son like a lamb, letting him get away with things. 10. She completely loses her temper; her mindless rage takes over until it burns out. In the process, she shames her son unmercifully. 11. He asks that someone else be given his scholarship; he pays for the dead hen; he tells his mother he will send money to pay her back for all she has done for him. 12. She feels that we must be extremely careful and very sincere about the choices we make, so as not to go against our destiny; that is, one must not try to force life into a particular direction. 13. and 14. Answers will vary and should be imaginative.

Page 29 The Chameleon
1. He wears a new greatcoat, and is followed by the constable. Moronoff carries a small package while the constable is charged with carrying confiscated berries. Citizens hide when they hear of Moronoff's approach. He takes command of situations and makes prejudicial pronouncements. 2. it is a small business district surrounding a square; the shops and taverns attract beggars; the language of the inhabitants betrays a lack of refinement or education. 3. because someone says the dog looks like General Tartaroff's 4. He is a man who is overly concerned with appearances. 5. to take the dog to the General and tell him that it was sent by Moronoff 6. Moronoff's only concern is the identity of the dog's owner. Does General Tartaroff own it, or not? 7. "No need to shiver, little chap! 'Grr-rrr' . . . He's angry, the rascal . . . the little scamp . . ." 8. Minor officials wish to be thought more important than they really are. In order to feed their own egos, they sometimes exploit those placed in their trust. Yes, people in every station in life throughout the world can fall victim to the same failing.

Unit 2 Modern Drama

Page 31 Twelve Angry Men: Act One
1. Answers may vary, but the fact that they are nameless probably helps us to focus on the *types* of men they are. Each one represents a different way of approaching the task they've been given.
2. Eight stands at the window after everyone has taken a seat; he must be called to the table.

3. He's nineteen years old; he's accused of knifing his own father; he lives in a slum; and his mother has been dead since he was nine. He's tough and angry.   4. The jurors react with a mixture of negativity and embarrassment. The stage directions give this information.   5. to convince Eight that they are right and he is wrong   6. that the burden of proof is on the prosecution   7. around midnight   8. the man who lived in the apartment below and the woman who lived across the street   9. eight o'clock   10. It helps bring out the facts as presented in the case. At first, things appear clear-cut, but as each juror brings up questions or concerns, our view alters. The reader is drawn into the case as one of the jurors.   11. "You're right. It's the kids. The way they are—you know? . . . Rotten kid! . . ."   12. He feels that the man hardly seemed interested and did not conduct a proper cross-examination of the witnesses. He did not ask the right questions.   13. that it is not really an unusual knife at all—any number of people might have one   14. Yes, because the other jurors have begun arguing among themselves; there are hints that Five and Nine may change their votes.   15. Answers will vary, depending on the juror chosen, but should be based on character traits revealed in the play.

Page 33   Twelve Angry Men: Act Two
1. They think it was Five; It was actually Nine.   2. He admires Eight's courage and feels he deserves support. He wants to hear more.   3. "She remembers the most insignificant details."   4. Three begins a game of tick-tack-toe.   5. It calls into question how he could have heard the boy say, "I'm going to kill you," as the train roared by.   6. He suggests that the old man lied because he wanted attention. He was a man who needed "to be recognized, . . . questioned, and listened to . . .," according to Nine.   7. Answers may vary. He probably feels that Eight gives persuasive reasons for discounting the significance of the boy's yelling, "I'll kill you." Perhaps he no longer wants to align himself with Ten and Three.   8. No, all that may have been proved is that if the boy did yell, the whole neighborhood would have heard it and that the threat may have been empty in any case.
9.

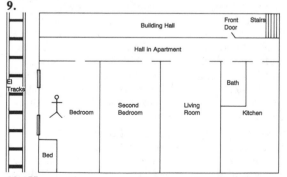
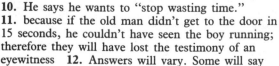

10. He says he wants to "stop wasting time."   11. because if the old man didn't get to the door in 15 seconds, he couldn't have seen the boy running; therefore they will have lost the testimony of an eyewitness   12. Answers will vary. Some will say

yes, Eight seems to be baiting and taunting Three, which is out of character for Eight. Others will say no, Three is overreacting in his usual way and Eight is simply responding to that.   13. Both acts end with Eight presenting information that throws new light on the case. In each scene one bit of supposed evidence is refuted or seriously questioned.   14. FOREMAN:Guilty; TWO:Not guilty; THREE:Guilty; FOUR:Guilty: FIVE:Not guilty; SIX:Not guilty; SEVEN:Guilty; EIGHT:Not guilty; NINE:Not guilty; TEN:Guilty; ELEVEN:Not guilty; TWELVE:Guilty—Answers may vary on FOREMAN, TWO, FOUR, SIX, and TWELVE.

Page 35   Twelve Angry Men: Act Three
1. Foreman, Three, Four, Seven, Ten, Twelve   2. He says, "I want to know who stands where." He wants to identify those jurors who are against him.   3. a. that the stabbing as the prosecution presented it—downward—was possible   b. that knife fighters do not use their weapons as Three described, but underhanded   c. because Five has seen many such knife fights   4. He feels that Seven is not taking his responsibilities as a juror seriously; that Seven is not making decisions based on conviction but based on convenience.   5. Nine men vote not guilty and three vote guilty.   6. People like this kid lie; they don't need a reason to kill; they get drunk and kill; most of them have no feelings; they're no good.   7. because it is the most damaging to the boy and, thus, the most dramatic to the play; it is the evidence that has convinced Four all along that the boy was guilty   8. Six   9. She testified to looking out the window while in bed to see the boy kill his father, but she wouldn't have been wearing her glasses in bed.   10. Ten looks down and shakes his head no.   11. He was once outspoken and sure; now he is beaten and silent. He is wrong and ashamed.   12. In Act Two; Nine comments that Eight has a great deal of courage to stand alone. (It is ironic that he addresses Three with these same words now.)   13. Answers will vary, but Three probably voted not guilty because he was afraid to stand alone in his decision. Also, he may have finally become aware that he was in fact wrong.   14. Each student will have a different answer.

Page 37   The Romancers
1. Sylvette is standing on a bench, leaning against a wall. Percinet sits upon this wall, reading to Sylvette. She "listens attentively."   2. She is uneasy about being with Percinet, and she thinks she hears someone who may discover them.   3. Answers should be something along these lines:
Percinet: OK. We'll stop here. I like this place. It's good for reading Shakespeare.
Sylvette: Yes. The poetry and the scenery go together. What makes it even better is the way you recite it.   4. In both cases, the parents hate each other (and forbid their children to see one another).   5. that she will keep away from the Bergamins   6. Sylvette was gathering nuts, and her ribbon blew away. Percinet climbed up on the bench to retrieve it, and Sylvette climbed up on the bench also.

7. He goes right along with them. Without missing a beat, Percinet is able to jump in and round out each of Sylvette's plots.   8. to the fact that Percinet has been reading plays ("In verse!"); he believes this has put Percinet's brain in a whirl   9. He threatens to remove all the greenery, remortar the surface, and put broken bottle ends on the top.   10. marry him off to a rich girl   11. They are both widowers, fathers of one child, and landowners.   12. They have been scheming to have their children marry one another.   13. Pomp and circumstance: **b.**; humorous: **a.**; Venetian: **e.**; classical: **c.**; gallant: **d.**   14. Yes; Percinet saves Sylvette from her abductors, just as they had imagined. Bergamin and Pasquinot come along in time to witness the heroic deed, just as they had planned. Straforel leaves his bill and should receive hefty payment, just as he had planned. The children will probably marry, the houses will be united, and all will live happily ever after—as planned.   15. Answers will vary, but will probably note that both pairs work together to deceive the other two. Sylvette and Percinet hide their love from their parents while Bergamin and Pasquinot hide their desire to see their children marry one another.   16. Answers will vary.

Page 39   Our Town: Act One

1. With the exception of placing Main Street near the back and the Gibbs and Webb households prominently in the foreground, Gibbs's on the left (actor's right) and Webb's on the right (actor's left), each student's mapping will be different.
2. He states that it is May 7, 1901. It is dawn, almost 5:45.   3. The Stage Manager knows not only about the past lives of the people in this play, but he knows what happens to them in the future also. He knows more about the characters' lives than they do themselves, and he can gather all of this information together and display it for the audience.   4. **a.** Joe had a very bright future as an engineer, but was killed in World War I.
b. Answers will vary. Most students will say it makes them sad, upset, even angry. Some may express regret and dismay at the waste of such a promising life. Others may comment that the young man's death seems to point out that much of what happens to us is beyond our control. Some may find the Stage Manager's remark, "All that education for nothing," provocative or callous.   5. They both: wake the children up; make breakfast; urge them to eat; admonish them to stand or walk properly (i.e., nag).   6. for Grandmother Wentworth's highboy; take her husband to Paris, France   7. objective; perhaps to emphasize that Grover's Corners has an existence and a history independent of the actions and emotions of the people we see on the stage   8. Belligerent Man:**b.**; Lady in Box: **a.**; Woman in Balcony: **c.**   9. Emily enjoys doing well in school; she likes giving speeches.   10. Answers will vary. Perhaps Mrs. Webb is being insensitive to a young girl's need to feel beautiful. Perhaps she feels that in such a small, ordinary town extraordinary beauty would be out of place. She is probably

telling Emily that she is pretty enough to become a wife and mother.   11. He wants to include a copy of this very play; so that people in the future will know what we were really like "in the provinces north of New York at the beginning of the twentieth century."   12. about the fact that George has not been chopping the wood   13. Simon Stimson's alcoholism   14. Descriptions will vary. Advantages might be such things as the close-knit community; open, friendly people who look out for one another; the absence of major violence or crime; and the scenic beauty. Disadvantages might be the lack of diversity in the people; the impression that everyone knows everyone else's business; the gossipy nature of the place; etc.

Page 41   Our Town: Act Two

1. Couples "marry young"; at approximately 18. ". . . just after High School Commencement. That's the time most of our young people jump up and get married."   2. Grover's Corners is losing its best baseball pitcher.   3. He was scared and thought he'd made a mistake. He thought his bride-to-be was pretty, but he felt she was a total stranger.   4. Answers will vary; the reasons are probably many. She doesn't want George to catch cold and cough during his wedding, as she states, but she also seems to need to exert her influence over her son on his last day at home. Also, nagging George is part of her daily routine.   5. ". . . never ask advice on personal matters."   6. to find out "how all this began . . ."; to find out *why* Emily and George decided to marry and "spend a lifetime together."   7. that young love is crazy; you're like a sleepwalker—you can't see or hear properly
8. She says he's changed; that he no longer speaks to people. She says he has become conceited and distant as a result of his success in baseball.
9. Emily is mad because George does not pay enough attention to her; he has failed to treat her as his *girlfriend*.   10. He tells her he's glad she said it. He says, "I'm going to change so quick—you bet I'm going to change." He takes her criticism as a sign that she cares for him.   11. He decides not to go to college; he mentions that it could be a waste of time and that his uncle may need him on the farm, but the real reason is his desire to be with Emily.   12. Answers will vary. George and Emily will probably feel confused as to whether they are doing the right thing. Their parents may feel confused about their children marrying so young. Others may puzzle over the meaning or importance of marriage.   13. He becomes upset, afraid of growing old. He suddenly feels as though he's being pushed into something he doesn't want.
14. She feels alone and angry. She wants to run away.   15. Answers will vary.

Page 43   Our Town: Act Three

1. a cemetery on a windy hilltop near Grover's Corners   2. He has come for his cousin's funeral and also to see his hometown.   3. Emily; she died in childbirth   4. from a legacy left by Mrs. Gibbs (extra points for those who indicate the money probably came from selling Grandmother Wentworth's highboy)   5. February 11th, 1899—

her twelfth birthday   **6.** No, with the possible exception of saints and poets.   **7.** Checks should appear next to letters **b., d.,** and **f.**   **8.** Answers will vary. "They" are certainly the living. What the living don't seem to understand is how important each moment of life is or what it means to be dead.   **9.** Although answers may vary, those that follow are common:

Dr. Gibbs: delivers twins; remembers his wedding; has lost his wife

Mrs. Gibbs: prepares the children for school; prepares George for his wedding; is dead (and prepares Emily for death)

George Gibbs: begins relationship with Emily; marries Emily; loses Emily

Mr. Webb: gives political and social report; gives marital advice to George; gives speech at his old college

Mrs. Webb: prepares the children for school; prepares Emily for her wedding (but not for marriage); prepares a "normal" birthday for Emily

Emily Webb: begins relationship with George; marries George; is dead (and revisits her home)

Simon Stimson: conducts choir rehearsal and goes home drunk; conducts wedding choir; is dead (and complains about life)

Mrs. Soames: gossips about Simon Stimson; attends the wedding; is dead (and still commenting on others' lives)

Howie Newsome: gives his regards to Doc Gibbs; gives "best wishes" to Webb and Gibbs families; gives his regards to Constable Warren

Constable Warren: discusses Simon Stimson's drinking; discusses George Gibbs giving up baseball; discusses rescue of Polish man

Unit 3 Poetry

Page 45   Phoebus and Boreas, The Stone, and My Father & The Figtree
Phoebus and Boreas

1. In Greek myths, Phoebus is the sun and Boreas is the wind.   **2.** as a month of changes in which "the sun shines fitfully" and for which we don't know how to prepare; "an uncertain time"
3. Yes, he has an "interlined cloak" and is well "fortified."   **4.** to blow so hard the man's cloak will come off   **5.** No, it blows the sails from ships and the roofs from houses.   **6.** by shining down gently, causing the man to remove his cloak

The Stone

1. He was struck by a piece of rock during a quarry blast.   **2.** The fool comes to give an unexpected blow that is just as quick, sudden, and thoughtless as the fall of the deadly stone.   **3.** carve a gravestone for her dead love   **4.** They make him very uncomfortable, plucking at his heart, causing him to lose his breath and to feel his blood run cold.
5. She sits quietly and stares at his hands.
6. with Death, possibly because they are both cutting a name upon a lifeless object—he on the stone, Death on the young woman's heart   **7.** She dies.

My Father & The Figtree

1. to all fruits but the fig   **2.** a fat, sweet fig hanging on a branch heavy with fruit   **3.** because she feels he starts a lot of things he doesn't finish (and dreams of that which he does not have)   **4.** He calls it "a figtree song."   **5.** Answers will vary, but should note that he has moved about quite a bit (possibly searching for something) and has probably finally found the place he will not leave—the home with the figtree.   **6.** Again, answers will vary. Perhaps they are tokens of Allah's blessings upon him in this new land, perhaps they are emblems of the sweetness of his former life.

Page 46   The Fox and the Woodcutter and A Poison Tree
The Fox and the Woodcutter

1. that he hide her among the fallen trees and not tell the hunter were she is hidden   **2.** He swears that he will not betray her.   **3.** He says he hasn't seen the fox but points to where she is hiding.
4. Answers will vary, but students should recognize Aesop's condemnation of hypocrisy.

A Poison Tree

1. Yes, he expresses the anger he feels toward his friend and represses the anger felt toward his foe.
2. It is constant; he nurtures his anger all day and night.   **3.** It is a bright, shiny apple.   **4.** Answers will vary, perhaps along these lines: He knows it belongs to the narrator and seems to want to get back at him. In addition, the apple is so bright and appealing that he probably wants to possess it himself.   **5.** He eats the apple and, because it is poison, he dies.

Page 47   I Wandered Lonely as a Cloud and The Crazy Woman
I Wandered Lonely as a Cloud

1. He is above it, looking down.   **2.** to the stars in the milky way; because they look and shine like stars and are equally abundant   **3.** the flowers
4. to feel or show cheer   **5.** "that inward eye"
6. The mood is one of quiet happiness or contentment in a remembered scene.

The Crazy Woman

1. Answers may vary, but May is thought of as a cheerful month, warm, pleasant, full of new growth and birds' song, while November, with its chilly, wet, and changeable nature, is thought of as rather dreary.   **2.** She does not feel gay and cheerful; she feels her sadness more akin to November.   **3.** terrible   **4.** Answers will vary. The woman seems to see the people who are critical of her as petty conformists who expect to hear singing only when it is pleasant.   **5.** Most students will agree she is not crazy; she simply wants to express her emotions in her own way.

Page 48   Hope and New Face
Hope
1. Line 1: hovers   Line 9: sprouts
   Line 3: shakes   Line 11: lives
   Line 4: drops   Line 13: runs
   Line 5: explodes   Line 15: inflates
   Line 7: sticks
2. Answers will vary. The movement of the lines back and forth intensifies hope as something active. The lines have an organic, living look to them.
3. Line 17: gift   Line 21: God
   Line 19: argument   Line 22: serum
   Line 20: genius   Line 24: poem
4. Answers will vary. The block form suggests that hope is stable, solid, real.

New Face
1. honor it, examine the mystery, and know the feelings of it   2. mysteries, headless, rush of feelings, appears to be   3. an "inexhaustible spring" within the lovers themselves   4. Answers will vary, but may include observations along these lines: Love has made her a completely new person. She has never looked at anyone else with such powerful love reflected in her face before—thus it is a new face.

Page 49   To Julia de Burgos and Don't Ask Me What to Wear
To Julia de Burgos
1. a. You b. I 2. The lie is the rumor going around that Julia's poetry is giving Julia away.
3. in the way it reveals one's innermost feelings and personal observations
4. Answers may include any of the following:

I

essence   virile sparkle
truth   bares heart
gambles everything   life
strength   woman
belongs to no one/to all Rocinante
curled by wind
painted by sun

You

covering   frigid doll
falsehood   hypocrisy
selfish   grave
ladylike   belongs to husband
curls her hair   paints her face
resigned   meek
tied to prejudices

5. She feels disdain for her. The wife is "tied to the prejudices of men." Her husband is called her "master."

Don't Ask Me What to Wear
1. the mother of Cleis   2. Cleis is blond, while her mother is dark, as was her grandmother.   3. She tells her daughter to wear fresh flowers in her hair.
4. She doesn't seem to. The tone is rather one of admiration. She suggests flowers as the only suitable way to accent her daughter's beauty.

Page 50   The Zoo and Ordinance on Lining Up
The Zoo
1. caged in the zoo   2. to emphasize what God had intended for the lion had man not interfered
3. The lion eats him.   4. He pants in longing for and in vivid remembrance of his natural habitat, where it is hot.   5. Answers may vary along these lines: because he leads such an unnatural life; because he cannot do the very things that define him as a tiger—use teeth and claws to devour his prey—and so on.

Ordinance on Lining Up
1. to use "careful consideration"
2. moves quickly: R   one ends as a beggar: R
   is serpentine: R&L   moves without hurry: L
   one's beliefs become nonsense: L
3. No, there is "no changing from one line to the other"; probably because one is "an indispensable link" in the line one chooses.   4. Answers will vary. The poet's view certainly is not optimistic. It doesn't seem to matter what choices the individual makes—disappointment and heartbreak await everyone.   5. Answers will vary.

Page 51   Improved Farm Land and Six Haiku
Improved Farm Land
1. one half mile   2. a. Axmen and railsplitters cut trees and brush.   b. Stumps are dynamited and removed in wagons.   c. Plows cultivate the soil.
3. in that it now can be used to grow crops and raise livestock   4. Answers will vary; perhaps because tall trees seem to sing in the wind and they stand continuous through many generations, like a family.

Six Haiku
1. a. veiled b. dusk c. clouds
2. a. rain and whispers
   b. mosquitoes buzz and petals fall
   c. shower and sparrows grasping
3. Students should write haikus based on their impressions.

Page 53   Those Winter Sundays, Harlem, and Afterglow
Those Winter Sundays
1. for starting the morning fire and for his hard labor   2. He is probably a day laborer—he gets up early for work and labors in the "weekday weather," and his hands are "cracked."   3. When the house is warm and his father calls him.   4. with indifference or a lack of interest   5. Yes, he probably would. He now fully appreciates all the things his father did for him (in spite of the anger that may have existed in the family) and realizes they were done with love.

Harlem
1. put off to some later time   2. dry up, fester and run, rot and stink, crust and sugar over, sag, explode   3. Answers may vary. These are correct: "fester like a sore— / And then run," and "Maybe it just sags / like a heavy load."   4. Answers may vary. It could be that the dream itself explodes—leaving the dreamer wounded and scarred by its

impact. It could mean that the dreamer, overcome with grief and unfulfilled longing, explodes—causing destruction and injury.

Afterglow
1. the last glow of light after the sun has moved beyond the horizon 2. It turns the plain to rust.
3. Answers may vary. Fear seems to cause humans to hallucinate about the space. 4. to a person looking at the afterglow of sunset

Page 54 Sunset, The Naming of Cats, and For Anne Gregory
Sunset
1. a coin 2. It is setting. 3. the colorful sunset 4. It is the end of the day.

The Naming of Cats
1. a. a sensible everyday name that the family uses daily b. a particular name, one given to only one cat c. a name known only to the cat 2. in order for a cat to be able to "cherish his pride," or be proud of himself 3. thinking about his name

For Anne Gregory
1. her yellow hair 2. dye her hair; so she will be loved for herself alone 3. that only God could love her for herself alone and not her yellow hair

Page 55 The Traveler's Curse After Misdirection and The Fool and the Poet
The Traveler's Curse After Misdirection
1. The traveler has requested directions and been led incorrectly; he curses those who gave him bad directions. 2. It gets worse and worse as the poem continues, starting first with the wish that they stumble, then that they fall, then that a bone is broken, and finally that they break their necks.

The Fool and the Poet
1. Every poet is a fool. 2. You are the perfect example of the fact that not every fool who claims to be a poet is a poet. 3. No, his clever poem proves that poets are not fools. 4. Students will write various epigrams of their own.

Page 56 Sonnet 65 and On the Grasshopper and Cricket
Sonnet 65
1.
1: a	5: c	9: e	13: g
2: b	6: d	10: f	14: g
3: a	7: c	11: e	
4: b	8: d	12: f	

2. death 3. to a flower 4. by eroding them or causing them to decay 5. a coffin, or death 6. in that a hand can write strong and vivid verse—creating images of beauty that never die 7. In writing a poem describing his love's beauty, her beauty will live forever in the words he writes.

On the Grasshopper and Cricket
1. The first part is set in the summer heat; the next part is set in the cold of winter. 2. The Grasshopper sings in the mead (in a hedge, it seems); the Cricket sings in a stove. 3. Answers will vary, but may include that their songs are produced in warm, out-of-the-way places; also, they

are produced at rest and can be heard above all other sounds.

Page 57 A Round Shape Water Takes Inside the Gourd and In an Iridescent Time
A Round Shape Water Takes Inside the Gourd
1. the shape of whatever it is in or on 2. the individual 3. Answers will vary. The poem appears to have a more positive view of higher social classes. 4. √ Lie down with dogs, get up with fleas.

In an Iridescent Time
1. the narrator's mother and aunts; they are doing laundry 2. hearing 3. by using positive descriptive words: rainbow, honed, red 4. bees, wrens, Jersey calf 5. because the work being done is hard, rough work. However, the beauty of the day softens the work's roughness. 6. Answers will vary; perhaps to show that all four sisters were involved, all four working as one, in a unity of life, of effort, of love; perhaps to emphasize how diligent and thorough they were in their work. 7. the buzzing of the bees and the roaring of the calf

Page 58 By the Bivouac's Fitful Flame
1. in temporary encampment with the army, sitting near the flickering fire at night 2. It would illuminate its surroundings in an erratic manner, rarely holding anything in its light long enough for someone to see clearly or completely; the light would flicker and dance. 3. the speaker's thoughts—of life, death, home, and loved ones far away 4. Answers will vary. *Procession* has a militaristic ring to it—conjuring images of men on horseback in battle dress. It also evokes an image of a long line of people—a continuum of people—old and young, from past, present, and future. 5. fields and woods c.; darkness d.; a figure moving a.; shrubs and trees b. 6. comforting thoughts of the realities of the past before his wartime experiences, of those same realities which exist while he cannot be a part of them 7. "I sit on the ground. . . ." 8. winding, sleeping, moving, watching; answers will vary, but there seems to be a sense of time passing without beginning or end, in an eternal present

Page 59 Mrs. Kessler and Hortense Robbins
Mrs. Kessler
1. Mr. Kessler does not work, living entirely in the historical past; Mrs. Kessler does work, and lives in the present through the lives of others. 2. by studying their laundry 3. that they are not "prospering" but "falling back" 4. Answers will vary, but like Mrs. Kessler, life surely knows all of one's secrets; it also can be seen to drown people in sorrow, scrub the life out of them, and put them "through the ringer." 5. Answers may vary. The body prepared for a funeral is idealized, cleansed, the realities of its past hidden in order to present as perfect a public image as possible. Also, in the faces of the dead, one can see the toll the work of the "laundress, Life," has taken on them.

Hortense Robbins

1. the social elite, or the upper class 2. her social-butterfly existence, the fact that she was always traveling around the world 3. buried in the Spoon River graveyard 4. Yes, it is ironic that after years of frantic travel she must lie so still in the grave. It is also ironic that despite all her fame and wealth she is now forgotten, "No one cares. . . ."

Page 60 Samuel Gardner, Dow Kritt, and Cooney Potter

Samuel Gardner

1. He worked in a greenhouse and was probably a gardener. 2. Either or both of these would be correct: ✓ shady ✓ overshadowing. 3. The roots push it up to the trunk, branches, and leaves—the part of the tree visible above ground. 4. A tree's branches can "spread no wider than its roots."
5. Answers may vary, but he seems to be a warm and loving fellow, appreciative of Nature and her gifts. He is observant of the life around him and seems totally immersed in it. He is concerned with the deeper questions in life.

Dow Kritt

1. He dug ditches. 2. They both sprang from good seed, and they were planted at the same time.
3. Its roots have struck rock and can spread no further. 4. Answers may vary, but he seems to be a man who courts misfortune, whose limited, confined existence followed him from ditch to grave.

Cooney Potter

1. Although he inherited forty acres of land, he vastly increased his landholdings through his own efforts. 2. Not very well. He worked them from "dawn to dusk" and denied them things. 3. Higbee says Cooney died of smoking cigars. Cooney says he died of eating hot pie and coffee. 4. Answers will vary. Certainly smoking cigars could cause an illness, such as cancer, and death. Too much coffee can tax the heart and lead to health problems, also. Pie seems harmless enough, unless one overindulges and taxes one's heart by carrying too much weight.

Page 61 Oh, When I Was in Love with You and White in the Moon the Long Road Lies

Oh, When I Was in Love with You

1. being in love, or his love's influence on him 2. "And miles around the wonder grew" 3. probably his love, perhaps his reformed manners
4. Answers will vary according to each student's experience.

White in the Moon the Long Road Lies

1. Answers may vary, but the moon has always been a symbol of love as well as a beautiful ornament to lovers. Now that he is leaving his love, the moon has no meaning for the speaker. 2. The landscape is absolutely still; he is the only object in motion. 3. "The way will guide one back."
4. go far away, or circle the globe 5. He repeats them.

Page 62 When First My Way to Fair I Took and An Epitaph

When First My Way to Fair I Took

1. because he would stand for long periods looking at the things he could not afford to buy 2. "But where's the lost young man?" It suggests that much time has passed because he is so lost to the speaker that the speaker doesn't know what became of him—he is a distant memory. 3. Answers will vary. Rewrites should convey a sense that two plus two equals four (not five or three) no matter how we might wish it otherwise; likewise, the passing of time cannot be stopped or its effects changed.
4. because all humans experience the pain that results from lost youth, missed opportunities, and the changes and disappointments living brings (or words to that effect)

An Epitaph

1. a. It is getting dark; you should not stay here.
b. Your death is approaching; move on and live your life. 2. It seems as though he sighed, got angry, worried, complained, and grieved about his lot in life (something he no longer does). 3. It is a "balm for many fevers." He sleeps well in death, accepting his fate. 4. Answers will vary. Some students may see life as the "ancient evil," which can only be cured by the "balm" of death. Some may suggest that death is the "ancient evil," necessary to make life whole. It could also be offered, possibly, that life and death together constitute the evil—the pain and sorrow of one played against the stillness and darkness of the other.

Page 63 Hope Is the Thing with Feathers and The Grass So Little Has to Do

Hope Is the Thing with Feathers

1. Answers will vary. It certainly wouldn't be very poetic. The poet probably keeps the connection indirect in order to make hope into its own living thing, not just part of a poetic analogy. 2. because that is when it is most needed—when its song would bring the most comfort 3. keeps people warm 4. no, not even a crumb 5. Each student will record his or her own choice.

The Grass So Little Has to Do

1. stir to the breezes' tunes ✓ hold the sunshine ✓ bow to everything ✓ dwell in barns ✓ 2. "And make itself so fine, / A Duchess were too common / For such a noticing—"
3. The grass gives forth a perfume rather than a stench. 4. Answers will vary. Perhaps she wishes to be beyond death, resting in "sovereign barns" (an image of heaven). Perhaps she longs to be as close to nature (and as far from society) as possible—holding sunshine in her lap, feeling the soft dew, then dying and becoming a sweet-smelling part of nature. 5. personification

Page 64 What Mystery Pervades a Well! and A Thought Went Up My Mind To-day

What Mystery Pervades a Well!

1. Answers will vary. She sees the gleaming water, certainly, and perhaps her own reflection in it, when she peers into the well. The well itself is round and jarlike, a remote circle descending deep into the earth. 2. Answers will vary. Unlike the

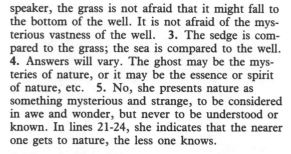

speaker, the grass is not afraid that it might fall to the bottom of the well. It is not afraid of the mysterious vastness of the well. **3.** The sedge is compared to the grass; the sea is compared to the well. **4.** Answers will vary. The ghost may be the mysteries of nature, or it may be the essence or spirit of nature, etc. **5.** No, she presents nature as something mysterious and strange, to be considered in awe and wonder, but never to be understood or known. In lines 21-24, she indicates that the nearer one gets to nature, the less one knows.

A Thought Went Up My Mind To-day
1. No, it has come only twice, separated by years. **2.** No, she knows not "where it went, nor why it came." **3.** Titles will vary. **4.** Answers will vary.

Page 65 The Road Not Taken and The Exposed Nest
The Road Not Taken
1. fall, or autumn **2.** "Because it was grassy and wanted wear. . . ." **3.** Yes, his exclamation, "Oh! I kept the first for another day!" indicates that he wanted to also travel the road he didn't take.
4. Answers will vary. There is some justification for all points of view. He seems resigned, but there is a tinge of regret also, and certainly the impression that he made the best choice is in evidence.

The Exposed Nest
1. The speaker sees someone (a friend) on hands and knees in the meadow. He thinks this person is trying to get the cut hay to stand up again. The speaker goes to help. He sees his friend holding fern, grass, and clover, and he sees a nest of young birds on the ground, unhurt but defenseless in the heat of daylight. **2.** the right to remain hidden and protected from the world's severity **3.** The mother might not continue to care for her babies if the humans interfere and change the natural environment. It could frighten her away. **4.** Answers may include: ". . . to do the best we could . . ." and "All this to prove we cared." **5.** The speaker does not know.

Page 66 Neither Out Far Nor In Deep, Desert Places, and The Secret Sits
Neither Out Far Nor In Deep
1. to abandon someone or something **2.** No, the speaker notes only the long passing of one ship and one standing gull. **3.** No, they don't look "out far" or "in deep." They are satisfied, however, that their limited perceptions are sufficient.

Desert Places
1. a field on a darkening, snow-covered evening
2. First *it:* the field; Second *it:* loneliness; Third *it:* loneliness (again) **3.** The speaker is not completely in touch with the depths of his own soul, perhaps ignoring it purposely to avoid fear.
4. a. overtaken by darkness **b.** ignorant or without understanding **5.** They are within him.

The Secret Sits
1. We dance in a ring and suppose. **2.** Answers will vary, we can only suppose. Perhaps it is the meaning of life, perhaps the meaning of death. (In any case, everyone gets their turn in the middle.)

Page 67 Half Moon and The Moon Rising
Half Moon
1. sight **2.** painting, photography, sculpture, silent films **3.** It would become more "realistic," losing its dreamlike qualities. The lapping of water, the wind, a frog croaking, might be added.
4. The frog sees the moon reflected in the water. It thinks it is a mirror.

The Moon Rising
1. Answers may vary. The moon appears to have taken away their ability to do what they are meant to do; they are denied meaning. **2.** Again, answers will vary. Living things would probably die. The heart represents life in a scene which has had life flooded out of it—it is totally alone. **3.** the sun, day, passion, etc. **4.** Answers will again vary; coldness, roundness, a silver color, a face; perhaps its freedom and raw power overwhelm any influence the coins have in the world—the moon is beyond ownership; or perhaps the coins cry for joy at the power of the moon.

Page 68 Pause of the Clock and The Guitar
Pause of the Clock
1. a sky full of stars, a ring-shaped galaxy
2. Their movement in time and space is so vast that a momentary "freeze" in our time cannot hold them back. **3.** the numbers on a standard clock face **4.** By using short, disconnected lines that do not allow a regular rhythm, the poem suggests a time which is being offset or is in disarray.

The Guitar
1. He repeats words and phrases using very short sentences. **2.** Answers will vary, but perhaps to avoid its being associated with or claimed by any individual. **3.** the five guitar strings, the guitarist's five fingers, or any relevant answer **4.** five times
5. "Weeping for things / far away." "Sands of the warm South / seeking white camellias." ". . . like an arrow without a target, . . ."

Unit 4 Legends of Arthur

Page 69 The Coronation of Arthur and from The Hollow Hills
The Coronation of Arthur
1. King Uther is Arthur's father. Upon the advice of Merlin, Uther turns his son over to Merlin to be raised by Sir Ector and his wife.

Queen Igraine is Arthur's mother. Arthur is taken from her as a baby.

Merlin foresees Arthur's glorious destiny and convinces Uther to turn Arthur over to Sir Ector and his wife. Merlin sees that Arthur is baptized and takes him to Sir Ector.

Sir Ector, loyal supporter of King Uther, agrees to take the infant Arthur and raise him as his own.

2. He must pull a sword from a stone and anvil.
3. The nobles protest that he is too young and not of noble blood. **4.** The common people demanded that Arthur be made king.

from **The Hollow Hills**
1. Merlin   2. Merlin, Arthur, Cei, Ector, Lot, Cador, and a hundred others   3. Macsen (Magnus Maximus)   4. Arthur

Page 70   The Lady of the Lake and Excalibur and Arthur Marries Gwynevere
The Lady of the Lake and Excalibur
1. King Pellinore; just as Pellinore is about to chop off Arthur's head, Merlin puts Pellinore to sleep and saves Arthur.   2. Excalibur is a magic sword found in the Lake of Avalon and given to Arthur by the Lady of the Lake.   3. When wearing the scabbard, Arthur will lose no blood no matter how badly wounded he is.   4. Merlin's prophecies are:
a. Arthur is about to challenge Pellinore.
b. Arthur's sister will marry Pellinore.   c. Arthur will receive a second magic sword.   d. The Lady of the Lake will give Excalibur to Arthur.
e. King Pellinore has fought Sir Egglame.
f. Excalibur's scabbard will protect Arthur from losing blood.

Arthur Marries Gwynevere
1. He tells Arthur that Gwynevere and Launcelot are destined to love one another, but that he will tell Gwynevere's father that Arthur wishes to marry her.   2. 150.   3. a knight as yet unborn, Sir Galahad   4. a. only to fight in just causes   b. at all times to be merciful   c. at all times to put the service of ladies foremost   5. Answers will vary, but given Merlin's prophecy that Gwynevere will love Launcelot, most students will anticipate trouble in the king and queen's marriage.

Page 71   The Tale of Sir Launcelot du Lake
1. He falls asleep.   2. He sees a knight follow three others on horseback, overcome and unseat them, then lead them away. He challenges the knight and is also defeated and led away.   3. Tarquine throws them on the ground, strips them, beats them, and locks them in prison with others he has captured.   4. He asks where he might go to find adventure.   5. his word that he will not try to escape   6. She will cast a spell that keeps him asleep, and they will take him to her castle. There he will be made to choose one of them.   7. Answers will vary, but Launcelot's honor would be stained were he to take up with one of the "lewd sorceresses."   8. He is "a good king and a true knight."   9. He unhorses five knights, breaking the backs of four of them, with one spear; he defeats Sir Madore, Sir Modred, and Sir Gahalantyne; then he unhorses another sixteen knights, then twelve more, each with one spear.   10. He says Sir Launcelot killed his brother, Sir Carados of the Dolorous Tower.   11. Sir Tarquine grows tired and lowers his shield. Sir Launcelot moves in quickly and drags Sir Tarquine to his knees. Sir Launcelot then unlaces Sir Tarquine's helmet and beheads him.   12. two days before Pentecost   13. the story of his enchantment by the four queens, and of his rescue by King Bagdemagus's daughter   14. Answers will vary; perhaps because, in spite of being defeated, they still admire Launcelot; perhaps it is too good a story not to tell; per-

haps because these knightly jousts are not taken very personally—somewhat like athletic games.

Page 73   from **The Once and Future King**
1. Probably not; Malory's Launcelot would have thought it unworthy to hide his identity or regret it in any way.   2. In a joust the knights fought one another singly, on horse or foot, for a prize. A tournament was more like a mock battle, with twenty or so men on each side rushing at one another.   3. "These mass battles were considered to be important . . ."   4. Probably not; merry England was filled with factions, hatred, feuds, battles, treachery, and extreme violence, as is Northern Ireland today.   5. White's Lancelot acts because it is "expected" of him, not because his noble or heroic character compels him; he seems almost reluctant to do it.   6. "There is no need to give a long description of the tourney. Malory gives it."
7. He thought it could cause bad feeling at Camelot.   8. four   9. Answers will vary, but there is certainly far less bloodshed. White's description may suggest that the numerous and terrible wounds inflicted by Malory's Launcelot were exaggerated for effect.

Page 75   The Death of King Arthur
1. Modred had prepared false letters recounting Arthur's death. Primitive communications and modes of travel made it extremely difficult to verify those assertions.   2. She goes to the Tower of London with loyal nobles and supplies and holes up there.
3. In threatening to excommunicate Modred to no avail and then fleeing for his life, the archbishop's actions suggest that the church had little power.
4. The people are fickle, and they use the excuse that Modred will bring them peace and happiness, while Arthur led them into war and want.
5. With a large army, Modred fights his own father for a crown that is rightfully his father's.   6. because they fought with the knowledge that their cause was the right one   7. because he feels he was wrong in his actions toward Launcelot—being spiteful and seeking revenge   8. to visit his tomb and offer prayers on Gawain's behalf, and to come to the aid of Arthur   9. He does as the dream has bidden him; offering a treaty to Sir Modred.
10. power over Cornwall and Kent and the right to succeed to the throne when Arthur dies
11. "Then, by chance, one of the soldiers was bitten in the foot . . . ."   12. four; King Arthur, Sir Modred, Sir Bedivere, Sir Lucas   13. He cares nothing for his life now that most all of his men are dead, and he may never have this chance again.
14. Arthur regrets the quarrel between Launcelot and himself over the love of Gwynevere.   15. Answers will vary, but should relate to what the sword represents. Excalibur is the symbol of the glory and power of Arthur and his court, and of England. Bedivere does not want it lost forever.
16. A hand appears and takes Excalibur, waving it three times, then disappearing.   17. to Avalon; for his wounds to be healed   18. to King Arthur's tomb "with fasting and prayers of contrition"; to the memory of King Arthur   19. Answers will vary. Arthur symbolized all that was noble, bold, and chivalrous in England. He also united many

different factions under his banner. He left the nation without a strong figurehead, and he was sorely missed. His subjects need to believe he will return to complete his work.

Page 77 from **Idylls of the King**

1. The old times were full of "noble chance" and daring knights, and all in Camelot seemed to glitter and dance. Now the knights are dead and Arthur soon will be. Camelot is in ruin, the country is no longer united under one great king. **2.** "an image of the mighty world" **3.** "The old order changeth, yielding place to new, / And God fulfils himself in many ways, / Lest one good custom should corrupt the world." **4.** Men are able to know God and pray "for themselves and those who call them friends." **5.** Answers will vary. Perhaps Arthur feels his failures may make him unworthy to enter Avilion; perhaps he believes he will die before reaching Avilion (and its healing powers). **6.** It has continuous good weather and lush vegetation; it is a place of happiness, beauty, and healing.
7. He stands for a long time watching the barge as it recedes into the distance, thinking about the past. **8.** Answers will vary. Dawn represents a new day, or a new beginning. Arthur's death is the end neither for England nor for himself. England lives on, and with it, the memory of King Arthur.

Unit 5 Experience in Short Fiction

Page 79 The Necklace

1. ". . . she allowed herself to marry a petty clerk in the office of the Board of Education." **2.** grace, beauty, charm, finesse, elegance, and wit **3.** She thinks about the beautiful houses and objects of the rich, about the splendid trappings of their wealth.
4. frocks and jewels **5.** She throws the invitation on the table. She feels she can't go because she hasn't a proper dress. **6.** natural flowers, two or three roses **7.** a necklace of diamonds ✓
8. "All the men noticed her, asked her name, and wanted to be presented." **9.** She sees that the necklace is gone. **10.** He retraces their steps, goes to the police and cab offices, and puts an ad in the papers offering a reward. **11.** He instructs Matilda to write a note to *Madame* Forestier saying that the necklace clasp had broken and that it was being repaired. **12.** He uses all their savings and borrows the rest to buy a thirty-six-thousand-franc necklace that looks like the one his wife lost. **13.** She is unhappy that her friend didn't return it sooner.
14. "They sent away the maid . . ." **15.** ten years
16. She now seems old. She is hard, strong, and crude. Her appearance is no longer of concern; her skin is weathered from hard labor; her general manner has become more coarse. **17.** She learns that the diamond necklace was not real—it was worth no more than five hundred francs. **18.** Students' answers will vary. Some may think that the shock of the discovery will be devastating to her. Others may believe that she has grown so detached from material things that whether the necklace had been real or not would no longer make any difference to her.

Page 81 The Interlopers

1. He is guarding his forest and hunting for a man.
2. Although well stocked with game, the territory in question is no more valuable than any other part of the Gradwitz forest lands. **3.** three generations—since the time of Ulrich's grandfather
4. Georg Znaeym **5.** ". . . the personal ill will of the two men." **6.** "The roebuck . . . were running like driven things tonight; and there was . . . unrest among the creatures . . ."; also, ". . . there was a disturbing element in the forest. . . ." **7.** Yes, he thinks it is his enemy, Georg Znaeym. **8.** Yes, they are constantly antagonizing each other and probably go out of their way to encounter one another. **9.** Lightning strikes a tree near them, and part of the tree falls on the two men, pinning them down. **10.** They taunt each other and claim they will "fight this quarrel out to the death." **11.** He offers the flask to Georg. **12.** He refuses the offer, saying he can't see because of the blood caked around his eyes, and that he wouldn't drink with Ulrich in any case. **13.** "Neighbor"; he wants them to end their feud and become friends.
14. He agrees. **15.** ". . . peace among the forester folk." **16.** They call for help together. **17.** nine or ten **18.** no one's men—they are wolves
19. Student opinion will probably range widely. It would probably not be as effective, because the sense of irony would be lost.

Page 83 The Man from Kabul

1. five years old **2.** Answers may include: chattering, stole, embarked, darting, playing, drumming, ran. **3.** He is a writer. **4.** He is walking slowly, wearing loose, soiled clothes and a turban. He has a bag on his back and holds boxes of grapes. **5.** children **6.** "Abdur Rahman, the Russians, the English and the Frontier Policy"—political issues of the day in India **7.** She clings to her father in fear and refuses the nuts and raisins offered by the Kabuliwallah. **8.** He listens patiently to Mini's chatter. **9.** Students' answers will vary. Some may feel that, because he was an author, Mini's father was fascinated by the interaction between two such oddly matched characters. **10.** Father-in-law's house means, literally, the home of a bride's husband—the place she will live (at one time to the exclusion of her own family)—and, figuratively, jail. **11.** He is like a "vegetable," only writing about action and travel. **12.** She is suspicious of him; she fears he may kidnap Mini.
13. He had been trying to collect a debt. The buyer refused to pay, saying he had not bought the item, and Rahman struck him with a knife.
14. She asks, "Are you going to your father-in-law's house?" He replies, "That is just where I am going, little one!" **15.** He asks to see Mini, the "little one." The father tells him there is a ceremony in the house, and he can see no one. **16.** the handprint of a child **17.** He says, "Little one, are you going to your father-in-law's house?" She blushes and bows her head, but she does not respond. **18.** He is sad that she does not eagerly greet him as she always had in the past, and he is saddened by the realization that his own daughter

will now be older, also, and may greet him as Mini has. **19.** Answers may vary, but should observe that the story is best told from the father's point of view because he is the person in the best position and with the most obvious inclination to observe all aspects of the friendship between his daughter and Rahman.

Page 85 A Letter to God

1. Lencho lives in the only house in a valley on top of a low hill. The house is shaped like a short pyramid, and from it one can see meadows, the river, the pasture, and fields of corn. **2.** Yes, Lencho sees all the signs of a good crop for the current growing season. **3.** No, he fully expects the rain to come. **4.** to coins **5.** because the rain makes the crops grow, and good crops bring money **6.** acorns, silver coins, and icy pearls **7.** Both silver coins and pearls are very valuable; the irony is that they are robbing Lencho of his crops, and thus the income he needs for his family. **8.** No. He says, "Let's hope it stops soon." **9.** He is left without food for his family, without crops, and without money to prepare for next year's planting. **10.** the help of God **11.** He decides to write a letter to God. **12.** a hundred pesos **13.** They laugh and think it amusing, but the postmaster is impressed by Lencho's faith. **14.** He decides to send Lencho money. **15.** No, he is not surprised. He is angry to find that all the money is not there. **16.** He is accusing the very people who helped him get the money of being dishonest. **17.** Students' answers will vary. Perhaps he felt that God might not have the leisure to listen to a prayer, but would certainly read a letter. Perhaps he thought such an important request should be submitted in writing. **18.** The postmaster believes that God is so unlikely to answer this sort of prayer that any tangible response at all will be viewed as a great miracle. **19.** Lencho is so certain that he has made a legitimate request to God, and that God will do something about it, that to receive less than his full request can mean nothing other than the intrusion of a human.

Page 87 The Sentimentality of William Tavener

1. She is smart ("a good manager"), opinionated, rather bossy, sharp of tongue, eager to give advice, and slow to forget another's errors. **2.** He is a good farmer, hard-working, grave, and strong enough to let his wife have her say. Hard toward his neighbors, he is even hard on his sons. He is "grasping, determined, and ambitious." **3.** He pays little attention to it—"His calm, clean-shaven face betrayed no sign of concern." **4.** to someone who chooses to disregard storm warnings until the storm is actually upon him **5.** almost an hour **6.** William will not allow the boys to go to the circus. **7.** They've worked hard and should be treated as well as the hired hands. The family can afford it. The boys need encouragement. They've never seen a circus, and need the experience. **8.** Because their rural upbringing may exclude them from certain cultural pursuits, Hester wants them to avail themselves of any opportunity to

broaden their horizons. **9.** an elephant, six parrots, a lion, monkeys, and two camels **10.** It wasn't two camels; it was one camel and a dromedary. **11.** He had earned some money, and he slipped away to the circus without his father's knowledge. **12.** during long sermons at prayer meetings **13.** As William tells his story, she draws her chair closer to him and leans her elbows on the table. As he continues, she draws her chair still closer to him. **14.** Their talks were almost exclusively concerned with money. She became her sons' defender against her husband. They had almost forgotten that they had ever had a closer relationship. **15.** It reminds them that they had at one time enjoyed life with each other, sharing common interests and experiences. **16.** neighbors, old friends, picnics, weddings, baptisms, parties, and things they did in their youth **17.** He goes to his secretary, unlocks it, and takes out ten dollars, which he puts on the table next to Hester. **18.** She takes mosquito netting from a basket and places it over William's head. Then she listens to him breathing. **19.** She had long been their defender against a husband about whom she felt "defensive and almost hostile." Now she feels a deep tug of loyalty toward William, so much so that her sons can sense that in future disputes she may join forces with her husband against them.

Page 89 The Rocking-Horse Winner

1. luck **2.** that "at the center of her heart" she loved no one **3.** They read it in one another's eyes. **4.** They live beyond their means. They have a nice house, servants, and they live in style, but they don't have enough money to keep it up. **5.** "There *must* be more money!" **6.** She says it's because his father is unlucky. **7.** "God told me." **8.** to take him to where there is luck **9.** He calls him "a perfect blade of the turf." **10.** Daffodil **11.** three hundred pounds **12.** fifteen hundred pounds **13.** He says, "It's as if he had it from heaven." **14.** "... I don't know.... I'm sure ... that's all." **15.** He hopes the house will stop whispering. **16.** They deposit it with the family lawyer, who tells Paul's mother it is from a relative. She will receive one thousand pounds on her birthday for five years. **17.** Answers may vary, but should include the observation that she badly wants to be first in something and has not succeeded, or that she makes considerably less money than her friend who works there, or both. **18.** She buys furniture, hires a tutor for Paul, buys flowers in the winter, etc. No, she spends extravagantly; there is "a blossoming of the luxury" Paul's mother had been used to. **19.** They are worse—they "trilled and screamed in a sort of ecstasy." **20.** his wooden horse **21.** Paul, frantically rocking on his horse **22.** He falls to the ground, unconscious with "some brain fever." He never fully regains consciousness and dies in the night. **23.** "poor devil" **24.** Answers will vary. Certainly, he felt the need to quiet the voices, which clamored for money. In his mind, money and luck went hand in hand, so he had to find luck to get money. Both his uncle and Bassett played the horses and helped him have access to the racetrack and the money that good luck there can bring. Then, too, Paul desperately wanted to help his sad, cold, despairing mother. Money may have been the only thing he felt he could give her to earn her love.

Page 91 The Needle

1. They were arranged by fathers, mothers, and matchmakers. 2. She would drop in on the prospective family early in the morning. If things were not in order, "that was it." 3. luck 4. She is beautiful and sophisticated, with smooth white skin. She speaks many languages, plays the piano, and is decorous and proper. 5. He is like his mother. He is handsome, clever, and learned, with dark hair and fair skin. 6. She looks for brides for her son. No, they all have some defect. 7. nobility of character 8. She does excellent needlework and has a good head for business.
9. Zamosc 10. Her black eyes burn like fire, and she is hot-tempered and crude. 11. Her eyes are as green as gooseberries, and she is as fresh and natural as they are. 12. ". . . the same law applies to a penny as . . . to a hundred guilders. Besides, today you buy a needle and tomorrow you may be buying satins for a trousseau." 13. her daughter-in-law
14.

✓ she becomes ill	✓ untrue stories are told about her
✓ she cries night and day	✓ the store begins to fail
✓ she acquires a bad name	

15. List may include two of these: She miscarries three times, becomes a hypochondriac, her mother dies, she swallows a needle (or thinks she has), her father dies, she never has children. 16. The girls become polite because they do not wish to spoil the chance of a good marriage by inhospitable attitudes. 17. She seems to feel that it has little effect. She says, "The truth is that everything is fated from heaven." If you are not destined to have or do something, you will not have or do it. 18. their names; because the girls *as individual persons* are not particularly important to Esther Rosa; she can learn what she needs to know about them through their behavior and is not interested in their names until she has made her decisions

Page 93 The Rat Trap

1. He makes rat traps, begs, and steals. 2. that the world is a large rat trap 3. It gives him pleasure to think of the people caught in the trap and "of others who were still circling the bait." 4. He is treated very well—given porridge, tobacco, and a place to sleep. 5. He smashes the crofter's window and steals his thirty kroner. 6. He feels pleased at having outsmarted the crofter. 7. the forest 8. He hears the strokes of a hammer at the ironworks; he walks in the direction of the sound.
9. He looks to the blacksmiths much like others of his type—long beard, dirty, and ragged. 10. He ignores the vagabond and adopts a superior attitude toward him. 11. because the ironmaster is a fine gentleman and might give him some money

12. He is alarmed and fearful. He thinks it would be like throwing himself "into the lion's den."
13. She has come to fetch the vagabond home with her to share their Christmas Eve. 14. that he is some kind of criminal and is on the run 15. He says, "Why the devil did I take that fellow's money?" 16. He realizes the vagabond is not his old friend. 17. She is saddened to think he will not be able to share Christmas with them. She wants him to enjoy a day of peace. 18. sleeping and eating 19. He says nothing, only staring at her "in boundless amazement." 20. that a man with rat traps had robbed one of the old crofters 21. a rat trap containing three ten-kroner notes and a letter of thanks from the visitor 22. He signs himself *Captain von Ståhle* because Edla has treated him as though he *were* a captain—he sees that in her eyes he is a man worthy of the respect and kindness offered an old friend. His action of returning the money he has stolen also makes him feel noble and worthy of her friendship. It is the action of a man who can proudly call himself a captain.

Page 95 Enemies

1. Answers may include: It is protected by high walls, is hard, cold, dark, stony, old, proud, and separated from things around it. 2. He stows her cases within her reach, packs her glasses, and sees to it that she has her proper pills. He takes down the folding table and buys her magazines. 3. No, he just does his job in a detached manner. He responds to Mrs. Hansen in kind, and cares about her as little (or as much) as she cares about him.
4. Some may say Alfred, because Mrs. Hansen is leaving and the two friends alluded to may offer an interesting tale. Others will say Mrs. Hansen, who is described so vividly in the first paragraph.
5. "She looked like a pudding that had risen too high and run down the sides of the dish." 6. her real self and her aging self 7. She is seventy-one.
8. Yes, she feels she is always alone but not necessarily lonely. Aloneness shields her. 9. because the food cannot be transported to her compartment and still remain hot, and because she doesn't like to dine in the same small space in which she will sleep 10. ". . . with the distant patience of an adult giving half an ear to a child." 11. To talk about them is to be proud or at least conscious of them. In either case, it is an admission of growing old. 12. ten or eleven months 13. The other woman has daughters and grandchildren. Mrs. Hansen has a son but she has disowned him. She says she has no children. 14. groans and the tinkling of a spoon being dropped 15. She assumes the woman is suffering indigestion due to overeating. 16. She died. 17. to Alfred; it says "It was not me." 18. Clara Hansen's "real self" is the image she has of herself as a young, vital, self-possessed woman. It is, it would appear, an idealized version of herself. Her "Old Fool" self is the 71-year-old woman she is afraid she will be mistaken for—a person of emotion, with needs, longings, fears, etc. She fights to supress the "Old Fool" and to remain controlled and aloof. She is afraid to let down her barriers and let anyone on the outside really know her, flaws and all. 19. Answers will

vary. She may really believe he will be concerned about whether she was the woman who died on the train. That she sends only one telegram—to her servant—indicates just how alone she is. It suggests that Alfred is the only person who will want to know she is safe. He will probably respond in the way he always has to his employer—with indifference.

Page 97 Action Will Be Taken

1. because he needs money **2.** Answers will vary; perhaps they suggest an atmosphere of goodwill and pleasure that he finds phony and unacceptable; he may feel the work place should be as dim and boring as the work that is done in them. **3.** He realizes that breakfast is part of the test, and thinks these actions will impress those in charge.
4. "pregnant with action" **5.** c. *Do you consider it right for a human to possess only two arms, two legs, and two ears?* a. *"How many telephones can you handle at one time?"* b. *"How do you spend your free time?"* **6.** He says, "The story of their lives is more important to them than their lives. . . ." **7.** Students should include one or two of the following: Broschek: Supports seven children and a paralyzed wife while working nights and handling four business agencies; passed two exams with honors in two years; never sleeps. Wunsiedel's secretary: supports four children and paralyzed husband while graduating in history and psychology; raises dogs and is a famous night-club singer. Wunsiedel: Displays driving energy, crying "Let's have action!" **8.** thirteen **9.** He drops dead in the narrator's doorway. **10.** He is holding two telephone receivers, writing with his teeth, and knitting with his bare feet at a machine under his desk. **11.** He is buried. **12.** because he has a pensive, inactive look and a face and form that go well with dark suits **13.** He is offered a job as a professional mourner with a "fashionable firm of funeral directors." **14.** He tells Broschek he never felt that he was working up to his capacity there, that his talents are being wasted. **15.** He feels he owes Wunsiedel for having found his "true vocation" as a professional mourner. **16.** He failed to find out what it was they produced there. **17.** Answers will vary, and one guess is as good as another, but perhaps it's because soap is such a universal product, an item modern industrial societies would be hard put to do without; perhaps because soap fits in so well with the clean, bright atmosphere of Wunsiedel's factory; perhaps because soap has a funny ring to it, etc.

Page 99 Miss Brill

1. a sophisticated, upper class—"Powdered with gold . . . like white wine . . . a glass of iced water"
2. a public garden in France **3.** She treats it with affection and appreciation, as if it were a living thing or a pet. **4.** During the off-season only "family," people who were always at the park, were there to listen. During "the Season" the band is playing for "strangers," visitors or tourists.
5. He scrapes his foot and flaps his arms like "a rooster about to crow." **6.** to listening to the conversations of others; she is expert at "listening as though she didn't listen, at sitting in other people's lives . . ." **7.** She gives them her complete attention, hearing every detail of the most mundane conversations. **8.** She watches the people.

9.
little girls ——————— like a young hen
little boys ——————— little French dolls
little children ——————— with big bows under their chins
high-stepping mother ——————— swooping and laughing

10. She thinks there is "something funny about . . . them." They are odd, silent, and old. **11.** because of the way people make entrances and exits as the band's "background music" changes to accompany the action; Miss Brill sits and watches it all as she would a play, "front row, center"
12. She thinks the band is responding to the scene between the woman in the ermine hat and the man in the gray suit, in which she appears to be rebuffed by him. **13.** She realizes that she too has a part in the play—that she comes every Sunday to be part of the performance. **14.** "as though it were the manuscript of her part . . ." **15.** start singing **16.** No, their dialogue comes as a shock; they are insulting and laughing at Miss Brill. It is as if the actors were insulting and making fun of an eager audience. **17.** She does not stop at the bakery for a slice of honeycake. **18.** Answers will vary, but most will agree she will probably not wear the fur again. She has heard the disparaging things the girl said about her fur, calling it a "fried whiting." Additionally, it seems as though the fur is "crying" in its box, almost as if it knows it will not be coming out again. **19.** Observations will vary.

Page 101 Tuesday Siesta

1. They are mother and daughter, dressed in mourning clothes. The girl is twelve years old, and the woman seems too old to be her mother. They are very poor. **2.** When used in the context of clothing, *severe* refers to simplicity of design, without decoration, plain. **3.** It is hot and close, the "still air . . . like tanned leather." **4.** A crowd has gathered, and a band is playing. **5.** Answers may include: put on her shoes, comb her hair, do whatever she needs to do now, don't drink the water later, and don't cry. **6.** It is Tuesday; August.
7. Answers will vary. There is a sense of things going to seed or being untended. People seem to have withdrawn from the town. **8.** eleven and "a little before four" **9.** to the parish house, or priest's house **10.** "The train leaves at three-thirty."
11. She wants the keys to the cemetery so that she may visit the grave of the thief, Carlos Centeno, who was her son. **12.** An elderly widow named Rebecca shot him with a revolver. **13.** "Ah, Mother." **14.** She explains to the priest that her son boxed to bring home what little money they had. She also told him never to "steal anything that anyone needed to eat," and he didn't. **15.** Because a crowd is gathering outside, presumably to see the woman whose son was shot as a thief.
16. They leave the parish house and go into the street, on their way to Carlos's grave. **17.** Answers will vary. They may feel they have nothing

to hide or to be ashamed of. The mother knows her son to have been a good man despite what he did. She is a proud woman who is determined to finish what she came to the town to do—before the three-thirty train leaves.

Page 103   The Demon Lover

1. Answers may vary; included may be: clouds piling up ink-dark, broken chimneys and parapets, unused channel, unfamiliar queerness had silted up, a cat wove itself in and out, no human eye, unwilling lock, warped, dead air.   2. Answers may include two of the following: the yellow stain on the mantelpiece, the ring left by a vase on the escritoire, the bruise in the wallpaper, the claw marks on the parquet floor.   3. The cracks are the result of the bombs dropped on London during World War II.   4. a letter addressed to her   5. because the house is closed up and the post office redirects all mail to her address in the country   6. to her bedroom   7. Answers will vary. It seems to be from an old lover.   8. a forty-four-year-old woman, dressed rather carelessly, with a thin neck and a tick to the left of her mouth, wearing a pink wool jumper.   9. a cut on her hand made by the breast button of his uniform   10. He is difficult to describe, as the author does not paint a very clear picture of him. He has intense, glittering eyes, but his face is never described. He speaks without feeling or much kindness.   11. wait   12. Answers will vary. Some may say that its sinister aspect involves expecting someone to wait unmarried so long for the possible return of a fiancé. Others may say that a promise that seems to involve remaining true beyond the grave, is certainly a sinister one.
13. No, not until she is thirty-two, and William Drover comes courting.   14. It is "a cracked cup from which memory . . . had either evaporated or leaked away."   15. call a taxi   16. She cannot recall his face; she will not know him when she sees him.   17. She heads toward the thoroughfare and the taxi.   18. a taxi   19. She screams, and beats her hands on the glass.   20. Answers will vary. It seems to be her fiancé—and perhaps he was the incarnation of death all along. He has finally come to take her with him to the land of the dead, so it would seem.

Page 105   The Masque of the Red Death

1. The following should be checked: dizziness, sharp pains, bleeding, sudden onset, dissolution, scarlet stains.   2. Victims are shut out "from the aid and from the sympathy of [their] fellow men."
3. in an attempt to keep out the contagious "Red Death"   4. to grieve or to think   5. five or six months   6. tall, narrow Gothic windows; the glass of each is colored according to the color of the room   7. Its ceilings, walls, and carpet are hung with black velvet. The windows are blood-red instead of a matching color for the furnishings as in the other six suites.   8. Braziers of fire mounted on tripods in the corridors shine through the windows.   9. It was "ghastly" and made those who entered look wild and strange.   10. "which embrace three thousand and six hundred seconds of the Time that flies"   11. grotesque, glare, glitter,

piquancy, phantasm, unsuited limbs and appointments, delirious fancies, madman fashions, beautiful, wanton, bizarre, terrible, disgust   12. Answers will vary. The word *writhing* suggests movement that is painful or uncomfortable. It is a word often associated with mental anguish also. In addition it has something reptilian or wormlike about it. This is not a jolly group.   13. He is dressed like a corpse; he is the image of the Red Death—the very thing they are furiously scrambling to avoid.
14. Prospero is so angered that he demands the man be unmasked immediately and then hung at sunrise.   15. The intruder's movements are deliberate, stately, slow, solemn, and regular; those of the Prince are rushed and hurried, impetuous.
16. He cries out, drops the dagger, then drops dead.   17. They are in "despair," and summon "wild courage."   18. They find it intangible; it has no substance.   19. They all die.   20. A plague, the Red Death, has killed many, and Prince Prospero decides to ensconce himself and his followers in an abbey far removed from the deadly disease. After a time, he decides to have a masked ball. Everyone dresses in brilliant but bizarre costume, dancing frantically to forget the pestilence that looms outside their walls. Into the revelry comes a tall, gaunt figure dressed like a victim of the Red Death. The guests are horrified, Prospero is enraged, and the intruder calmly, slowly walks through the hall. Prospero rushes after him, about to stab him, but falls to his death. The others rush at the intruder, try to grab his mask, but find it has no substance. They all fall dead.   21. Answers may vary, but the theme seems to be that there is no escaping death.

Unit 6 Shakespearean Drama

Page 107   Julius Caesar: Act One

1. to lead the others and wear out their shoes in order to get more work, and to see Caesar and rejoice in his victory   2. because Caesar's triumph comes as a result of the death of Pompey's sons; they had cheered and honored Pompey as they now support Caesar   3. to go home and weep enough tears to raise the water level in the channel
4. They leave quietly, without giving any response.
5. to take down the ceremonial decorations and drive the commoners from the streets; they want to check Caesar's ambition   6. He tells Caesar to beware of March 15. Caesar calls him a dreamer and walks on.   7. Brutus thinks of himself as less lively and outgoing than Antony.   8. He tells Cassius that it has nothing to do with him, that he is at war with himself.   9. "And since you know you cannot see yourself / So well as by reflection, I, your glass, will modestly discover to yourself / That of yourself which you yet know not of."
10. physical weaknesses   11. Answers will vary. Some will say that physical weakness merely reveals Caesar's humanity, that he has flaws and makes mistakes like any other man, and may still be an inspirational leader. Others may feel a man seeking to rule an empire should be above all reproach—should be stronger, braver, more intelligent than those he leads.   12. Brutus says he will consider

carefully all that has been said, and will listen to all Cassius has to say . . . if it is for the good of Rome. **13.** They look angry and upset. **14.** He wants fat, balding men around him—men who are not hungry for power but content and complacent. They are not "dangerous"; they will not thwart Caesar in any way. **15.** because men like Cassius cannot stand seeing someone who has risen higher than they **16.** Casca thinks the whole affair was foolish, contrived flattery, a public show to win common approval for a political move which has already been decided. **17.** epilepsy **18.** He will forge messages in different handwritings that acknowledge Brutus' worthiness and hint at Caesar's dangerous political ambitions, and throw them in Brutus' window. **19.** Answers should include two or three of the following: He has seen a slave whose hand was on fire yet it did not burn or pain him; he has seen a lion who looked at him and did nothing; he has seen women who swore they saw men walking in flames; he saw a night-bird during the day. He thinks they signify disaster for Rome. **20.** Caesar **21.** crown Caesar king **22.** He blames the people—the Roman citizens—who allowed him to gain such power. **23.** Brutus **24. c.** Caesar **d.** Antony **b.** Brutus **a.** Cassius

Page 109 Julius Caesar: Act Two
1. that he will abuse the power given him and scorn those beneath him **2.** "If the redress will follow, thou receivest / Thy full petition at the hand of Brutus!" **3.** to a rebellion that causes turmoil in a country **4.** dangerous, monstrous **5.** He feels an oath is unnecessary—the abuses they see occurring around them are enough to hold them in strong resolve. If not, they should all go home and accept tyranny. **6.** With Cicero among them they will not be considered young hotheads. His age and good judgment will give them respect in the eyes of the people. **7.** He feels that Cicero will not agree to join a movement that others have begun. **8.** spare him; he feels killing Antony would be a bloody deed ill thought of by the people; Antony is merely Caesar's follower—he will be powerless once Caesar is dead **9.** Cassius **10.** to tell him he is a man who is not swayed by flattery **11.** that Brutus tell her what is troubling him **12.** that soon he will tell her the "secrets of my heart" **13.** Calpurnia becomes concerned that so many supernatural omens are being brought to her attention in regard to Caesar's welfare. Portia's concerns are the product of a wife's observation of her mate. **14.** "Danger knows full well / That Caesar is more dangerous than he." **15.** that he isn't coming because he doesn't want to: "the cause is in my will" **16.** She dreamt she saw a statue of Caesar pouring fountains of blood, and Romans came smiling to bathe their hands in it. **17.** He tells Caesar it is a good omen, signifying that all Romans shall gain strength from Caesar. **18.** a paper that gives the names of all the men plotting against Caesar **19.** how Brutus is, what Caesar is doing, and what men are with him **20.** Portia: Sensing that her husband, Brutus, is about to do something deeply troubling, she tries to induce him to talk

about it. Calpurnia: Responding to bad omens and a terrible dream, she is convinced that Caesar must not go to the Capitol. She tries desperately to convince him to stay home. Artemidorus: He writes Caesar a note telling him that his closest associates are plotting against him.

Page 111 Julius Caesar: Act Three
1. No, he is shoved aside. **2.** Metellus asks Caesar to repeal his brother's banishment. **3.** Caesar's response reveals that he is beginning to take his political "divinity" seriously—he has risen so far above his fellows that he resides in the sky, comparing himself to the constant north star and to a god on Mt. Olympus. **4.** Casca is the first; Brutus the last. **5.** Perhaps Caesar feels that if the noble and patriotic Brutus would betray him, then all of Rome must desire Caesar's downfall. **6.** "Peace, freedom, and liberty!" **7.** as the "men that gave their country liberty" **8.** He believes they have killed a great and noble man to fulfill their pleasure. He is ready to die at their hands also. **9.** a place in the new government **10.** to hunters, or to princes who hunt for sport **11.** Antony wants to take his body to the marketplace and speak at a funeral for Caesar. **12.** Cassius wants to forbid it; he is afraid Antony will move the people. Brutus says he will explain why Caesar was killed, then announce Antony's speech, saying they have permitted it and that lawful burial rites will be given Caesar. **13.** The conspirators will be punished, and Caesar's death shall be avenged. The land shall be cursed; civil war will follow. The destruction will be so hideous that acts which now seem cruel will be taken for granted. The death toll will be enormous. **14.** his love; his fortune; his valor; his ambition **15.** He will kill himself. **16.** Antony states that all he has come to do is state the facts, the reality, of Caesar's life and of his relationship with the Roman people. In doing so, he does, in fact, seem to disprove what Brutus said. **17.** They are beginning to be sympathetic. **18.** He wants them to be eager for it, to demand it, to be ripe for action when they finally do hear it. **19.** Brutus turning on Caesar and stabbing him **20.** He says, "O, what a fall was there, my countrymen! / Then I, and you, and all of us fell down." **21.** No, it's exactly what he *is* doing—very successfully. **22.** They take Caesar's body to the holy place to burn it; with the fire they will burn the conspirator's houses. **23.** The people have taken affairs into their own hands, and irrational acts of violence begin to occur unchecked by Roman officials. **24.** Students' answers will vary.

Page 113 Julius Caesar: Act Four
1. No, Antony has begun to think of the Roman world as belonging to him, something to be divided at will. He states that each member of the triumvirate has a "share" in the "threefold world." **2.** Antony will see to it that undesirable policies and questionable activities are attached to Lepidus; Lepidus will be used to channel adverse public opinion away from Antony and Octavius. **3.** an ass, a horse, and personal property **4.** It has

cooled. Brutus feels that Cassius has become a fair-weather friend. He is confused as to Cassius' cool behavior. **5.** "When love begins to sicken and decay, / It useth an enforced ceremony." **6.** He doesn't want the troops to see that their leaders are at odds. **7.** because Brutus ignored his pleas for leniency on behalf of Lucius Pella **8.** Brutus accuses Cassius of being greedy, of using his influence and strength for personal gain. **9.** that they killed Caesar for supporting dishonest men, and that they cannot be involved in similar injustices **10.** He refused to send Brutus the money he needed to pay his men. **11.** Cassius is disturbed that Brutus has not overlooked the faults of a friend, but makes them out to be worse than they are. Brutus does not forgive and forget. **12.** his heart and his life **13.** Answers will vary. Perhaps he is intended to be comic relief, perhaps his remarks are meant to offset the emotional scene between Brutus and Cassius, perhaps it is meant to illustrate that Brutus and Cassius can be as contemptuous and offhand in their dealings as Caesar was in his. **14.** Portia is dead. She killed herself by holding hot coal in her mouth until she suffocated. **15.** They have had one hundred senators executed. **16.** The inhabitants near Philippi have only given grudging aid to Brutus' forces; they cannot be considered allies. When the enemy marches toward *them*, the citizens will join Antony, providing fresh troops and supplies. Brutus, on the other hand, notes that the forces and morale on his side can only decline from this point on. **17.** Brutus seeks company; he calls officers to his tent to stay the night; he asks for music and a book. **18.** Answers will vary. Perhaps it is because it was Brutus' evil doings that made Caesar a ghost, perhaps because some of the same corrupt attitudes that brought Caesar down are now a part of Brutus' character as well, perhaps because Caesar wants to do evil to Brutus. **19.** Answers will vary. Some will note that both men are proud and quick-tempered. Both consider themselves excellent soldiers. Both are apt to treat people with some measure of unconcern, if they do not fit into the personal vision each has for the immediate future.

Page 115   Julius Caesar: Act Five

1. Antony. Despite a show of will by Octavius, when it comes time for decisive action, he defers to Antony's judgment. **2.** Most students will agree that while Antony's account may be slightly exaggerated, it is fundamentally correct. **3.** Cassius apparently believes that events of such importance, events that affect the lives of so many, *do* bring down the supernatural upon them whether he would have it so or not. **4.** He finds suicide cowardly and abhorrent; people kill themselves because they are afraid of what might happen. He believes in waiting for the gods to decide when his death will come. **5.** "But this same day / Must end that work the ides of March begun . . ." **6.** Brutus begins to sense weakness in the forces of the triumvirate and sends dispatches calling for an all-out attack. Unfortunately, the attack occurs too soon; Brutus' army stops fighting to loot the fallen soldiers of Octavius. In the meantime, Antony sur-

rounds Cassius. Cassius sends Titinius to check their camp. His welcome is misunderstood as capture, and Cassius seeks for, and finds, his death at the hand of Pindarus. When Titinius discovers what has happened, he kills himself. A second battle begins. **7.** a sense of history, loyalty to his country, a willingness to protect his leader at all costs, a willingness to die with honor **8.** He asks both of them in turn to kill him. **9.** Brutus is so full of sorrow that he is crying. **10.** Brutus still believes he was right in joining the conspiracy and ending the tyranny of Caesar. Despite all that has happened, he holds to his original theory that Caesar's death will result in a better Rome. **11.** He has Strato hold his sword with the blade out, then Brutus runs into the blade. **12.** He is telling Caesar that he can now rest easy; Brutus is dying—and has killed himself more eagerly than he did Caesar. **13.** because Brutus, alone of all the conspirators, did not kill Caesar out of envy but because he believed it was in the interest of the common good **14.** and **15.** Answers will vary.

Unit 7 Nonfiction

Page 117   The Secret Room

1. The author describes the mood in negatives, as the opposite of the sunny spring skies and the flowers in the lamppost boxes. **2.** The song is Holland's anthem. **3.** automobile motors **4.** She will not let go of her suitcase. **5.** "In this household," Father said, "God's people are always welcome." **6.** ration cards **7.** He is being carefully watched by the Gestapo. **8.** She is not completely certain that Koornstra will be sympathetic to her cause. **9.** He tears the "continuing" coupon from each ration card. **10.** Corrie and her family know half the people in Haarlem, and she believes that God will let her know which ones can be trusted. **11.** She is impressed by such distinguished guests, but more than anything, she is overwhelmed by the aroma of real Dutch coffee. **12.** "Their chief work, I gleaned from bits of conversation . . . ." **13.** Smit **14.** because of the odd-placed landings and the different floor levels of the two houses, one in back of the other; it is easy to build a secret room that will fool people, and if more houses were built this way, more people could be safely hid **15.** "Wood sounds hollow. Hear it in a minute." **16.** This question should have particular appeal for the more visually oriented students. **17.** Answers will vary. She loves her country, but patriotism seems less a factor than religion, in this rather religious family—brother a minister, nephew a church organist—though opening the door to the first fugitive seems simply the action of a generous and basically courageous spirit. Also, her sister Nollie was already harboring two fugitives.

Page 119   I Escape from the Boers

1. "It was necessary to hit off the exact moment when both their [the sentries'] backs should be turned together." **2.** "Whether the sentries would challenge or fire depended entirely upon their individual dispositions, and no one could tell what they would do." **3.** "Failure being almost certain, no odds against success affected me." **4.** Answers will vary, but an exhausting list can be found in the paragraph on page 613 beginning, "I walked on leisurely through the night . . . ." **5.** "I saw with relief that the railway ran steadily towards the sunrise." **6.** "I had been able to take very little exercise during my month's imprisonment . . . ." **7.** "I looked around and saw here and there the lights of houses and thought of the warmth and comfort within them, but knew they meant only danger to me." **8.** He hides Churchill in abandoned mine workings. **9.** Howard's two Dutch servants are suspicious of the amount of food being consumed in his home. **10.** "Rather than face this ordeal I would much have preferred to start off on the veldt with a pony and a guide . . . ." **11.** The need for concealment and deception gives him a feeling of guilt and undermines his self-confidence. It is a passive role quite different from the active role on the battlefield. **12.** six **13.** He imagines the pleasures of freedom, a successful escape, and rejoining the army. **14.** He is afraid his snoring might give him away. **15.** nearly three days **16.** The Consulate secretary gives Churchill a hard time because he is an unexpected visitor. **17.** Answers will vary, for they depend on the student's own fears, experiences, and self-image.

Page 121 By Any Other Name

1. "Oh, my dears, those are much too hard for me." **2.** The girls' father "had a tour of duty to perform" in that area as an officer of the civil service (and their mother is not well). **3.** They were educated at home by their mother. **4.** She feels as if Cynthia were another personality for which she has no real responsibility. **5.** Indian: wide verandas and central courtyard; British: dark brown paint and matted floors **6.** Answers will vary. Santha is shy; she is confused; she is rejecting her assigned name. **7.** She lightly touches Santha's arm. She doesn't smile. **8.** Yes. The school lessons seem "babyish" to Santha. **9.** She has been taught at home that the youngest should be allowed to win. **10.** Rather than attempting to win when she is able, she lets younger students win instead. **11.** sandwiches **12.** "inattentive . . . only half listening to the teacher" **13.** Answers may vary. It seems the cultural differences are too great, and the superior attitudes of the English are a barrier. **14.** Answers will vary. She may think Santha is too young to understand. Premila is probably too angry and frustrated to talk about it, and may want to speak to her mother first. **15.** dusty hedges, thorns in the ditches, fragrance of the eucalyptus trees, women in pink and green silks, people carrying baskets of vegetables on their heads, the heat, being tired **16.** Answers will vary. She seems torn between her inability to continue as her children's tutor and their need to develop a sense of self-worth as Indians. **17.** "It had all happened to a girl called Cynthia, and I never was really particularly interested in her." **18.** At first Premila wants to be accepted by the other children by behaving as they do; she tells Santha to go and sit with her class and not to run to greet Ayah. Later she is

much offended by the assumption that Indian children cheat and wants nothing more to do with the school. **19.** Answers will vary. It is easier to make Indians as British as possible than to attempt to appreciate their uniqueness and learn their ways.

Page 123 First Lady Under Fire

1. She continues to spell Dolley with an "e," betraying her rural roots. **2.** Men and women were treated as equals and were encouraged "to oppose moral complacency and inhumanity wherever they saw it." **3.** the death of her first husband **4.** "By charity I mean generosity of spirit. It was, I believe, the secret of Dolley's charisma." **5.** tactful, pleasant, warm, friendly, good memory, delightful, outgoing, and other similar words **6.** "There was no hope of getting additional funds because the nation was by now perilously close to war." **7.** Federalists are pro-British. They feel that the war is the President's conflict; they point to early defeats as proof of his foolhardiness. **8.** ". . . the capital was an emotional, gossip-ridden city." **9.** Madison's Secretary of War disregards the President's orders to defend the city. **10.** Word spreads that two British deserters have revealed that their army is stronger than the American force. **11.** "Perhaps simply surviving one panic is the best recipe for dealing with the next one." **12.** She removes the presidential papers from their residence to render them unavailable as a source of British propaganda. **13.** She orders the servants to prepare a formal dinner. **14.** Answers will vary. "She was appalled by the thought of leaving the father of the country to the mercy of the enemies he had once defeated." **15.** The people were aroused to greater war effort. Many volunteered to finish the building of Fort Greene in Brooklyn. **16.** Dolley Madison is a person of good feeling, as well as courage. Her generosity of spirit, her belief in the goodness of most people, and her ability to use these qualities in the role of First Lady can be considered a kind of genius. **17.** "Like most courageous people, Dolley Madison had acted out of an inner sense of what was right." The author thinks that Dolley Madison has no way of knowing the effect of her rescue of Washington's portrait. But just as in her role as White House hostess she has "a knack for saying the right thing at the right time," she also has an instinct for taking the right things at the right time from the White House, as she flees.

Page 125 Four Letters
Dolley Madison

1. her sister **2.** "My friends and acquaintances are all gone—even Colonel C, with his hundred men, who was stationed as a guard." **3.** She doesn't want to go until her husband comes and she knows he is safe. **4.** The portrait, the best-known one of Washington, hangs today in the White House.

Bartolomeo Vanzetti

5. He believes that they are persecuted for being "libertarians or anarchists." **6.** so that when Dante grows up he will know "how good and brave your father has been with you"; other answers are

also possible   **7.** "They would not even have convicted a leprous dog; not even executed a deadly poisoned scorpion...." "They would have given a new trial to a matricide and habitual felon...."
8. "be brave and good always"   **9.** Answers will vary, for they are purely a matter of opinion.

Anne Morrow Lindbergh
10. Their plane is being serviced.   **11.** "the poor monk who had a vision of an angel"
12. plateau   cotton wool
       ice   feathers
13. Indianapolis to St. Louis

Harry S. Truman
14. Yes. "I reared up on my hind legs and told 'em where to get off and they got off."   **15.** The U.S. will not continue to provide assistance as a Santa Claus would; Truman's first interest is the U.S.A.   **16.** The war with Japan must be brought to a conclusion. Britain and Russia must fight alongside the U.S. in its war with Japan.
17. "I'm sick of the whole business—but we'll bring home the bacon."   **18.** informal, tough, down-to-earth, feisty, outspoken, unafraid, ordinary—a common man who uses common language and common expressions, such as "reared up on my hind legs," "the old man," and "bring home the bacon"

Page 127   Three Days to See!
1. "I have often thought that it would be a blessing if each human being were stricken blind and deaf for a few days at some time during his early adult life."   **2.** "through mere touch"   **3.** "If I can get so much pleasure from mere touch, how much more beauty must be revealed by sight."
4. "laughter, sorrow, and many other obvious emotions"   **5.** Vision allows one to "grasp quickly the essential qualities of another person by watching the subtleties of expression, the quiver of a muscle, the flutter of a hand."   **6.** Answers will vary.
7. Answers will vary.   **8.** the faces of dear friends and a baby; books; her dogs; woods; sunset
9. She has never been able to recognize the approach of dawn. She has never seen the sun.
10. the world, past and present: museums of art and natural history; movies or the theater   **11.** Homer was blind.   **12.** The "static grace" she has felt by touching statues of dancers has led her to imagine the beauty of dance.   **13.** the "workaday" world: the city; slums, factories, parks, the foreign quarters; a funny play   **14.** "the colors of women's dresses moving in a throng"   **15.** "Always my eyes are open wide to all the sights of both happiness and misery so that I may probe deep and add to my understanding of how people work and live."
16. Most normally sighted people take their vision for granted because they cannot comprehend not being able to see.   **17.** "Use your eyes as if tomorrow you would be stricken blind." And apply the same method to other senses.   **18.** Answers will vary.   **19.** Each student will write a different itinerary.

Page 129   Grandmother Zabielska
1. "She was the first person whom they knew, whom they lived with, to leave this familiar life."
2. The age at which Grandmother Zabielska dies becomes the norm, just as the red line on a thermometer marks normal temperature. Anyone who dies before that age, dies too young.   **3.** "It was, like Grandmother's life, well balanced, Christian, conducted intelligently and generously."   **4.** She has never tried to deceive herself in the face of unavoidable events.   **5.** She is without complaint or nervousness, maintaining a gracious and grateful disposition.   **6.** They feel that the "straightforward manners" of the Zabielskis are somewhat unfeeling in the face of the death of a loved one.   **7.** She knows that she is not going to recover.   **8.** Basia keeps her cross-stitches straight in finishing Grandmother's tablecloth.   **9.** "She had her roots deeply in life." For Pani Liza it would be very hard to leave everything and everyone.   **10.** "When the dessert is to be passed, we don't want to go back to the soup."   **11.** "When we knew that something was bad, we simply tried not to do it."   **12.** Answers will vary, for this is a matter of opinion.
13. "She never lost her balance."   **14.** Each day the children are brought to stand for a while near Grandmother's bed.   **15.** They kneel around Grandmother's bed and recite prayers for the dying.   **16.** As a coffin is removed from the family home, it is lowered three times on each threshold, for the dead person to say goodbye to his or her house.   **17.** "in his house, among his own people"
18. Dying by man's hand could be "dreadful, cruel, and unnatural."   **19.** Answers will vary. It helped them realize that dying is a part of life which need not leave them terrified. Death is something simple and natural, to be faced reasonably and intelligently.

Page 131   The Day We Flew the Kites
1. The family takes seriously the biblical commandment to work only six days of the week.   **2.** The women are spring cleaning.   **3.** "It had been a long, hard winter, but today it was Spring."
4. No. The author's mother only admits that they will watch the boys "a minute." Mrs. Patrick is "laughing guiltily."   **5.** "God doesn't make two such days in a century."   **6.** Wishes written on slips of paper with holes punched in them are slipped onto the kite string. If a wish ascends to the top of the string attached to the kite, it will come true.   **7.** puppies   **8.** "The gulf between parent and child was greater then than now."
9. Several answers are possible. Everyone was very happy; parents and children seemed more equal; parents were less stiff and children less spiteful.
10. She has forgotten how the work left undone was attended to at the end of the day.   **11.** It probably made such a strong impression on everyone that they all locked it away; speaking about it would perhaps make it seem ordinary.   **12.** It was for her such a deep emotional experience that she feels a little ashamed. Also, she thinks her ideas about it were ridiculous.   **13.** Students' answers will vary. The author lives in a city apartment, has only one child, is less comfortable with her situation than her mother had been.   **14.** "It reminds

me of that day we flew the kites." **15.** This was the first time that anyone had mentioned that day, and so the memory she had locked up many years before could now come out and be shared with her mother, making them even closer. **16.** She has learned to take advantage of a beautiful day, even if she has many tasks to do indoors. **17. a.** ten years **b.** Students' answers will vary. Perhaps the author wishes to emphasize that the experience had such strength that time had not dimmed it for anyone in the family. **18.** In P.W. camp, thinking of kite-flying day reminded him that life in fact had been better at one time; it had been a time of freedom, without regimentation, without fear or uncertainty. **19.** the death of Mr. Patrick **20.** The day they flew the kites was a happy time and thus a happy memory, one that cheered her up despite her loss. Her husband had very much enjoyed that day. The author is glad that the day meant a lot to still another person.

Page 133 My Store of Grievances
1. **a.** WE'RE OPEN 24 HOURS A DAY AND WE HATE IT.
   b. OUR PRICES ARE HIGH AND WE DON'T CARE.
   c. WE'RE GOING TO CHEAT YOU, AND SO WHAT?
   d. OUTRAGED CUSTOMERS WILL BE ASKED TO LEAVE.
   e. EVERYTHING WE SELL COSTS TOO MUCH.
   f. WE FEEL THAT THE CUSTOMER IS A CONDUIT OF MONEY.
2. good service and low prices **3.** "Whether the customers do doesn't interest me." **4.** "It means we can cheat you however we feel like it."
5. **a.** 1: poor arithmetic 2: lack of skill at the cash register 3: time wasted with personal phone calls 4: lack of care about their jobs **b.** 1: adequate in math 2: trained at the cash register 3: not distracted by personal matters 4: caring about their jobs
6. Answers will vary. Often it is the minor annoyances which take the convenience away from the convenience store. **7.** Probably not; the outrageous comic approach suggests that no single convenience store could ever be quite this bad! **8.** It cares about their money. **9.** The clerk puts them "in a sack that's too small and rips open." **10. a.** "Now get lost." **b.** "Thank you and come again."
11. *Store* has a double meaning. For some time the author has been *storing* up his grievances against convenience stores, and now he has dreamed up a *store* that will express those grievances. **12.** Answers will vary. Most students will likely think it a good name, for it says what the author wants to say in order to make his point. **13.** Each student will compose a different list.

Page 135 Biographies Bring New Companions
1. Meeting people is one of the "pleasantest" ways of enjoying ourselves. **2.** No. Chute mentions soldiers, statesmen, writers, but never nonpublic figures. **3.** "It brings its hero as vividly to life as if he were standing in the same room." **4.** It is a

window into the life; the better the biography, the bigger and clearer the window. **5.** The reader of biographies "meets not only the people who are alive today but those who lived in all the past centuries." **6.** The biographer must re-create a living being from a mass of impersonal documents. **7.** "This sense of reality, of showing great people as they really were, is one of the best things about biography." **8.** A great man never gives in to "confusion and discouragement and a sense of defeat." **9.** Portraits or busts are static and "fix" a person in a moment of time; a biography can show the person developing over an entire lifetime. **10.** "A good biography takes away the sense of 'costume' that often blocks our imagination when we think about the past." **11.** "A good biography can destroy time." **12.** "Biography brings the times to life again . . . and it makes the world a more spacious and interesting place to live in." **13.** "It widens your sense of enjoyment over things that have nothing to do with books." **14.** They help the reader to understand that while he or she sees the greatness of a person in hindsight, the biographical subject often had to deal with a strong sense of inadequacy. **15.** Answers will vary. "Many people in his own day did not think Shakespeare's plays were very good." **16.** The reader discovers a continuity among and a kinship with "all the people in history who have made the world a place worth living in." **17.** Answers will vary. Chute doesn't seem to think so. **18.** Each student will list different autobiographical facts and give different answers to these questions.

Unit 8 The Novel
Page 137 The Pearl: Chapter I
1. Answers may include: roosters crowing, pigs turning twigs and wood, birds chittering, waves on the beach. **2.** Juana (Coyotito in his hanging box is also acceptable) **3.** the Song of the Family **4.** Yes, he is happy with his life. He feels quite fortunate in his wife and child, ". . . this is the *Whole*," he thinks, and he sighs "with satisfaction." **5.** "That was the only breakfast he had ever known . . . nearly killed him." **6.** the Song of Evil (later called the Song of the Enemy); the scorpion is moving toward Coyotito **7.** Juana is practical and efficient in her attempts to draw the poison from the baby's wound. While Kino had attacked the scorpion in a fury, she focuses on what needs to be done to deal with the reality of the situation.
8. Kino, Juana, Coyotito, Juan Tomás, Apolonia, all the neighbors and their children, and four beggars **9.** the race that has oppressed their people for nearly four hundred years **10.** Answers will vary, but some sense of the poverty and inequities of life in the town should be a common response.

Page 138 The Pearl: Chapter II
1. in that it magnifies some things and obscures others; things seen are unreal and untrustworthy; they have "the sharp clarities and the vagueness of a dream" **2.** The canoe represents a continuity with the past as well as personal property and a source of food. **3.** She prays for a pearl that they

can use to pay the doctor.   **4.** as luck, or a pat on the back from God, the gods, or both   **5.** the Song of the Pearl That Might Be   **6.** the fact that now the need is great to find the pearl, as is his desire to find it   **7.** that it will drive luck away   **8.** It is as large as a gull's egg, perfectly round, and silver.   **9.** The swelling in Coyotito's shoulder has subsided.   **10.** Answers may vary. It seems as though he is releasing his pent-up tensions and expectations in joyous exuberance. He is, certainly, overjoyed that Coyotito is healing and that he has found such a wondrous pearl. He is described, however, as howling and screaming, words that do not have particularly joyful associations. Perhaps, mixed in with the joy, is a feeling of anger that his well-being should hinge on a small, round bit of oyster residue. Perhaps he fears that the gods are only toying with him.

Page 139   The Pearl: Chapter III
1. The news traveled faster than people could tell it, reaching the village even before Kino and the other pearl fishers got home.   **2.** The shopkeepers hope to sell the clothing that has not been selling well. The doctor (who had refused to treat Coyotito) claims that Kino is one of his clients, and dreams of visiting Paris again.   **3.** The pearl becomes wrapped up in everyone's dreams. Kino is their enemy because he stands between them and the pearl.   **4. a.** a marriage ceremony in the church   **b.** new clothes   **c.** a harpoon   **d.** a rifle   **e.** an education for Coyotito   **5.** They will say that Kino spoke foolishly and that God punished him for stepping out of line. They will also say that they saw it coming.   **6.** He is old but sharp, and treats "these people" like children. He is condescending and speaks very formally. He expresses pleasure at the "good thoughts" of Kino and Juana.   **7. a.** scraping crickets   **b.** shrilling tree frogs   **c.** croaking toads   **8.** The gods dislike men's plans, wanting success to come by accident. The gods punish men who are successful through their own efforts.   **9.** a capsule full of white powder   **10.** He wraps the pearl in a rag, digs a hole in the corner of the house, puts the pearl in, and covers it with dirt.   **11.** Answers will vary. Kino says, "So the doctor knew," but is very suspicious as he remembers the white powder. Also, he again hears the evil music.   **12.** He offers to put it in his safe.   **13.** everyone   **14.** someone digging in the dirt floor for the pearl   **15.** He leaps out into the dark and attacks.   **16.** She wants to throw it away, smash, or bury it. She sees the evil it is causing people to do, and is afraid that it will come to destroy her family.   **17.** Answers will vary, but since Steinbeck is building his novel around an ironic usage of the Pearl of Great Price parable in the Bible, some students may be aware that somehow the greed, materialism, and cruelty the pearl brings with it are characteristics of the "world."

Page 141   The Pearl: Chapter IV
1. that Kino is going to sell his pearl today   **2.** They have fixed the maximum price they will offer Kino for the pearl.   **3.** They would do various charitable things with the money, such as giv-

ing it to the poor.   **4.** "How can we know what is a fair price, if we do not know what the pearl buyer gets for the pearl in another place?"   **5.** Kino didn't have the experience to know whether the doctor's treatment of Coyotito was trustworthy and his charges fair. He had to accept things on faith (and was cheated). The same holds true in his dealings with the pearl buyers.   **6.** The loss was punishment for trying to rise above their station.   **7.** Answers may vary, but he seems to be a shady character—one whose appearance and actions belie his true personality. Despite the outward look of sincerity, his hand practices illusion.   **8.** that it is a mere curiosity—too large and clumsy to be of value   **9.** They begin to believe the dealer, hinting that they suspected the pearl's flaws all along. (They think Kino should accept the thousand pesos.)   **10.** To speak of a plan implies a conviction to see it through.   **11.** "We survive."   **12.** Answers will vary, but may mention the pearl buyers, who know the enormous value of the pearl and are unscrupulous; the doctor, who is greedy and not above stealing; a neighbor, many of whom seem capable of rationalizing such a theft; or a thief hired by any of the above.

Page 142   The Pearl: Chapter V
1. She takes the pearl and runs to the ocean; she is about to throw it in the water.   **2. a.** reason   **b.** caution   **c.** sense of preservation   **3.** the pearl   **4.** She sees that many in the town are set against them now—twisted by greed or jealousy over the pearl. She doesn't think people will be able to see their way clearly to treat Kino fairly.   **5.** His boat has been destroyed—a large hole knocked in its bottom.   **6.** It is burned down.   **7.** to the house of Juan Tomás and Apolonia   **8.** leprosy   **9.** "This pearl has become my soul."   **10.** Answers will vary. His need to keep the pearl, his "soul," is greater than any other need. He has become animal-like in his defense of it. His rage and the brutal attack of his wife, therefore, are the reactions of one whose entire being is centered on protecting something that she has stolen from him. Then too, Kino may be seen as one attempting to define himself as a "man." Juana, in attempting to destroy something that he feels defines his manhood, becomes his enemy.

Page 143   The Pearl: Chapter VI
1. It is an ancient animal thing out of the past (perhaps a surfacing of his animal instincts as well as a spiritual link to the wisdom and courage of his people).   **2.** the song of the pearl and of the family   **3.** He says they would not have tried to steal the pearl if it were of no value.   **4.** Instead of:

a. a rifle	Kino sees: a dead body with a bleeding throat
b. a marriage in church	Juana crawling with her face beaten
c. Coyotito learning to read	Coyotito feverish from medicine

5. It has become sinister and is united with the song of evil.   **6.** They are looking for him.   **7.** He compares them to hunting dogs.   **8.** toward the mountains   **9.** He sees the defeat that he fears is unavoidable. His vision is very detailed, including the stones, leaves, and branches the men will investigate.   **10.** "No."   **11.** a small spring   **12.** The pools provide water to sustain wild animals, and they also provide a place for these same animals to eat their prey, or to be eaten.   **13.** by evening   **14.** to get the one with the rifle   **15.** Students' answers will vary; some may see the tragic conclusion foreshadowed in the story.   **16.** to a slow lizard (and later to a shadow)   **17.** a coyote pup; he shoots in the direction of the cry   **18.** a terrible machine   **19.** "The sun was behind them and their long shadows stalked ahead, and they seemed to carry two towers of darkness with them."   **20.** Answers will vary. Perhaps that they had suffered so terribly they could never suffer in this way again—they became numb to pain. Because Kino and Juana no longer feel pain they are, in some sense, above ordinary human experience.   **21.** a malignant growth   **22.** green; perhaps because it is a color associated with new growth and new beginnings; also, it offers a hopeful contrast to the gray, sinister nature of the pearl   **23.** Answers will vary, but should observe that this kind of knowing is deep and intuitive, embedded in the "soul" of Kino and Juana and their people.

Page 145   Master and Man: Chapters I, II, and III

1. December; the 1870s   **2.** Russia   **3.** $5,000   **4.** He is a peasant of about fifty. He is hardworking, handy, strong, kind, and cheerful. He has been separated from his wife and two children for twenty years. The separation was due largely to Nikita's violence and irrationality when drunk. He has given up drinking.   **5.** Nikita had nowhere else to go and was in no position to demand an honest accounting from his master.   **6.** He speaks to Brownie as though he were human.   **7.** pale, thin   **8.** take Nikita with him; because he is carrying money and because he may need Nikita's help should the weather get worse   **9.** He fears Vassili will leave without him.   **10.** It is cold, windy, and snowy; visibility is poor.   **11.** because he believes that Nikita should be ". . . flattered at being talked to by such an important and highly-educated man as himself . . ."   **12.** He wishes her well and feels he has little to blame her for.   **13.** "the pursuit of bargains" (money would also be an acceptable answer)   **14.** Answers will vary, but may include that he is in a hurry to make the deal, so he chooses the quicker way. Also, he seems to enjoy overriding Nikita. Additionally, he seems to see himself as invincible.   **15.** the Zakharovek estate   **16.** The horse finds it.   **17.** stay the night in Grishkino   **18.** another sledge   **19.** Nikita: He is upset with the way the rivals drive their horse so unmercifully. Vassili: He is happy and lively as a result of their victory.   **20.** back in Grishkino   **21.** "It is nearly dark. You had better stay here."   **22.** Paulson's; it is the only book he owns   **23.** Students' answers will vary; most will foresee their continued journey (and hardships) into the frozen night.

Page 147   Master and Man: Chapters IV, V, and VI

1. It is still undivided between the family members.   **2.** He refuses, saying, "I would rather not. . . ."   **3.** The old man uses the word to mean "matter" or "affair," saying it could be a "terrible business" if the two men got lost. Vassili uses the word as he always does, to mean "commercial dealings."   **4.** the dividing of the land   **5.** No, he thinks, "Perhaps we shall never get there," but his passion for business overcomes his reason.   **6.** Nikita is a servant, long resigned to doing what others want.   **7.** right   **8.** "The willing, docile animal obeyed . . . although he knew that it was in the wrong direction."   **9.** He falls into the ravine.   **10.** Nikita "could hear Vassili's shouts and Brownie's welcoming neigh some moments before he actually caught sight of them."   **11.** return to Grishkino   **12.** Nikita is now making the decisions.   **13.** He is resigned—it is another one of those unpleasant circumstances in life over which he has no control.   **14.** Vassili uses his outer coat to make a shelter, then lights matches so he can smoke a cigarette.   **15.** Brownie's—because the animal is totally dependent upon him for his welfare   **16.** ". . . the making of money, and yet more money"   **17.** He sees her as a woman incapable of striking a profitable bargain.   **18.** a lumberyard   **19.** "I was a fool ever to have listened to Nikita."   **20.** Answers may vary, but Vassili's contempt seems to be a result of his philosophy, which equates human worth with the money and power they possess.   **21.** 1:10 A.M.   **22.** by thinking, ". . . it would be nothing for him to die . . . He has nothing much to lose . . . whereas I have much to gain. . ."   **23.** Answers may vary; however, it seems that in the midst of this blizzard, in the dead of night, his only sources of self-definition and power have lost all of their value. He can neither buy nor talk his way out of this danger; his power and prestige are meaningless.

Page 149   Master and Man: Chapters VII, VIII, IX, and X

1. Nikita views life from the perspective of a man who has always worked hard serving other men. He has begun to grow weary of this "ceaseless servitude." Death is "not particularly unwelcome." He sees death as the opportunity to serve a greater master, God, a master who will treat him well.   **2.** He was shouting to Vassili to leave behind the sacking so he could cover himself, since Brownie no longer needed it.   **3.** ". . . that there was One who could hear him and would never abandon him. . . ."   **4.** a tall piece of wood bending in the wind   **5.** that he has been going around in circles   **6.** "He felt sure now that he was to perish in the midst of this fearful waste of snow, and that nothing could save him."   **7.** his business dealings, his possessions, and lastly, his son   **8.** Answers will vary, but may include the observation that to Vassili religion is another bargaining tool—one expects help and comfort in proportion to one's "payment" in candles, prayers, and abstinences. He sees these things as only relevant to his old, well-ordered life—religion offers him no comfort now.   **9.** back

to the sledge **10.** He disentangles Brownie and makes the horse as comfortable as possible.
11. "Pardon me, for Christ's sake." Nikita is asking for forgiveness. At that moment, Vassili realizes all for which he needs to be forgiven. He sees the shallowness of his life. **12.** He covers Nikita with his own body to keep him warm. **13.** a feeling of great joy **14.** Answers will vary. Possibilities include: "I would have died never really having lived." "I would never have known what caring and goodness felt like." "I would not have known the joy of giving." **15.** "Has he come yet, Mikolovna?" **16.** Students' answers will vary. Some may say it is Vassili's "better self"; some may point to the capital "M" and say God; some may specifically mention Jesus Christ because the Man calls for an act of self-sacrifice. Vassili says to him, "Yes, I will go!" and "I am coming!"
17. The burden is Vassili. It becomes heavier be-

cause a weight of snow is being added to the dead weight of his master. The weight could also represent his servitude under Vassili. **18.** Vassili has died. **19.** Answers may vary, but he doesn't seem to have changed. He is the same good man—a survivor and a pragmatist. He had been good enough and selfless enough to act as the catalyst for his master's transformation. **20.** twenty years
21. Nikita dies at home, an old man, in peace, surrounded by his family and the comforts of his religion. **22.** The title is subject to a number of interpretations, including the possibility that the "Master" of the title is Vassili and the "Man" his servant, Nikita. Then too, the Master may be seen as God, with Man being all human beings made in His image. The master/man concept can also be seen to exist in one person—an individual, or man, can be "master" of his or her own fate or of his or her own beliefs and actions.